HELL
DIVERS

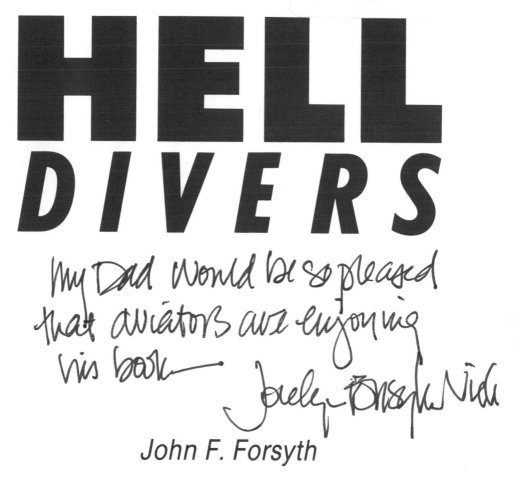

My Dad Would be so pleased
that aviators are enjoying
his book —
Jocelyn Forsyth Nick

John F. Forsyth

Motorbooks International
Publishers & Wholesalers ®

First published in 1991 by Motorbooks International Publishers &
Wholesalers, P O Box 2, 729 Prospect Avenue, Osceola, WI 54020 USA

Motorbooks International books are also available at discounts in bulk
quantity for industrial or sales-promotional use. For details write to
Special Sales Manager at the Publisher's address

Library of Congress Cataloging-in-Publication Data
Forsyth, John F.
    Hell divers : Navy dive-bombers at war / John F. Forsyth.
        p.   cm.
    ISBN 0-87938-493-X
    1. World War, 1939–1945—Aerial operations, American.   2. World
    War, 1939–1945—Naval operations, American.   I. Title.
D790.F59 1991   90-48366
940.54'4973—dc20   CIP

On the front cover: A Confederate Air Force SB2C-5 being flown by
Nelson Ezell, who also restored the airplane. *Michael O'Leary*
On the back cover: Author John F. Forsyth in his heavy shearling flight
jacket in 1944. *USN*

Printed and bound in the United States of America

Contents

Preface

Most of this book was written forty-four years after the events it chronicles. The stories are all as true as human memories can be.

The events I recount were not unique to me. Every pilot and gunner has his own stories, many strikingly similar, and all as good as or better than mine. I wish I could tell all their stories, and I hope they will forgive me for writing in the first person and understand that writing, even my own version, was not easy.

My first regret is that I could not find and print pictures of all the players and in their planes or flight gear, pictures of us as we were. I especially regret not being able to include pictures of our captains in combat, Mark Eslick, Jr., and George D. Ghesquiere, and if I could, I would show you Charlie Gold, our first skipper, and William Ellis and Wilson Coleman, our air group commanders.

Most deeply, I regret not introducing more material on the rest of Air Group 18—the torpedo squadron and the fighter squadron. We worked and fought with them. We relied on them. We admired their courage and determination. Daily they risked their lives for us. If chapters are to be written, they each deserve a book. Speaking for the bombing squadron, I say, "Gentlemen, we salute you!"

Acknowledgments

It is with great pleasure that I acknowledge the help of Phyllis Luxem, without whose steady encouragement (and slashing red pen) this book might never have been completed.

I relied heavily for comment, corroboration and pictures on the airmen and pilots of VB-18, including especially Russ Bourne, Jim Chaney, Art Chauvel, Art Daschke, Ben Emge, Don Freet, Dick Masterson, Pat McGovern, Ben Preston, George Searle, Dick Shipman and Don Wilson.

Dick Masterson has written a readable, historically correct booklet on the squadron. It was helpful to me. I recommend it to you.

I thank John Gilman for letting me tell his story and Larry Sowinski of the Intrepid Air and Sea Museum in New York City and Robert F. Dorr, both of whom supplied many of the photos used. I thank Mary Bragg and Barbara Harris for endlessly retyping and for great patience; Louis Banks, Ray Nugent and Isabel Stanley for their comments and encouragement; and Cheryl Drivdahl for superb editing.

I am most grateful to Greg Field of Motorbooks International for his enthusiastic response to my manuscript and help along the way.

Introduction

World War II was a tremendous emotional experience, for both those at home and those at the cutting edge. Its truths are beyond fiction. It was adventure, sense of great mission and tragedy of the highest order. It brought out the very worst in people and the very best in people.

Chronicles and histories of battles are necessary but it was the daring deeds, the awful tragedies, the bright courage, the adventure, the selflessness and the emotion of the people involved that created the stories that are handed down from one generation to the next.

This is a story of our airmen that I wrote to share with my squadron mates. Our common experiences, our peril, and our reliance on each other for another day's life forged an uncommon bond between us.

The stories are first for them, so that they, as I, can live again the best of the things we did and so that they, as I, can say to their families, "This is what it was like. This is what I did, which I have never told you about."

Second, this writing is to share the sensation of intense flying, combat flying, with all men and women whose imaginations soar and whose heartbeats quicken at the adventure and excitement of flying or for whom the history of World War II is a forever fascination.

One theme in this book is that war is an unacceptable solution to our problems, and we must develop other solutions quickly, now!

Peace with freedom and human rights has a price. The price is less than the cost of war, but it is harder to pay because the emergency of war may seem distant. If we do not provide for our own defense war may not be that distant. No matter how we deplore it we must be ready to cope with the presence of powers in the world that seek out and devour or subjugate the weak. History is full of extreme examples—for instance, the disastrous Pilgrimage of the Virgins.

In more recent times there was no way to appease Hitler, and when his armies rolled into the lowlands in 1939 we had no force or way to oppose him, let alone stop him.

In the beginning we lost thousands of our best and bravest airmen, soldiers and sailors because we had not kept up our defenses and especially our weapons. As we tried to mobilize and resist, we had no soldiers. As we began to draft our men, we had no arms for them; soldiers drilled with pieces of wood for guns. When first we sent our airmen out to resist the Japanese our aircraft were hopelessly outclassed by theirs.

Consider the pilot who, at the beginning of the war, took off in an outdated, inferior plane to fight Zeros, knowing he had almost no chance of surviving, but willing to give his life just to slow the tide so we could arm and defend ourselves. How do you justify to his wife and child our sending him out to his death with inadequate weapons?

Former-President Ronald Reagan has shown us again that we can reduce world tensions when we move from strength. Let us never forget that, because if the "next war" comes there will be no time to rearm and catch up, as we did at the start of World War II.

Chapter 1

Sinking the big ship

We sank a ship, a big ship, a battleship, the biggest battleship the world has ever seen.

Her name was *Musachi*, and she had a twin sister, the *Yamato*.

They were built in secrecy in Japan, behind high walls in violation of all treaties. To prevent discovery, the workers lived for years behind those walls, completely cut off from the rest of Japan. The twin vessels were built to be the biggest and most powerful ships in the world. They were.

On a day in 1943, a submarine on patrol near Honshu cautiously raised its periscope to scout a Jap task force. The sub saw a battleship so large as to border on the unbelievable. It ducked and beat it, but the word of a monster on the loose was out. The information trickled down through the fleet, and for months, when wardroom conversation lagged, someone would mention the name *Yamato*, and the stomachs of all would tighten at the thought of the great behemoth on the prowl.

I was a dive-bomber of Bombing Squadron 18, on board the *Essex*-class fast carrier *Intrepid*. We flew SB2Cs, the big, chunky Curtiss Helldivers. We

Curtiss SB2C Helldivers. USN

were a typical group of Navy pilots, some of us eager and ready to go and some of us not so eager but ready to go.

There were fellows like George Searle, who was usually found immersed in a Damon Runyon book or explaining in Harry-the-Horse's Runyonese 10,000 reasons why he would rather be back in the States. George considered himself well adapted to flying multiengine airplanes and extremely ill suited for flying single-engine airplanes thousands of miles from land, straight down on some of the emperor's very best ships, and we agreed with him to the extent of calling him Multiengine George.

The USS Intrepid. USN via Intrepid Museum

The real worth of a man comes out in combat. George received a new name one day, on a scouting mission in his dive-bomber. He was accompanied by a lone fighter—primarily, we dive-bomber pilots always felt, to report where we were killed if the pair was jumped by Zeros. George was heading, with plenty of misgivings, in the direction of Manila Bay. The bay was then a hotbox, raided only once by Navy planes and no place to be poking around alone.

As George bored in on the bay, two Jap warships—a cruiser and a destroyer—were driving hard across the bay, hell-bent for the open sea. They bristled with guns and were directly between the heavy antiaircraft (AA) defenses of Corregidor and Bataan, both guarding the entrance to the bay. Multiengine George saw them and threw away the book. He was a dive-bomber, and spell it any way you like, that meant only one thing to Searle—"dive."

Down he went, throttle jammed to the firewall, one plane against the flame-spurting cannons and machine guns of two big ships and two forts. He had no right to live. He planted his big bomb on the cruiser's deck, saw tracers zip through his wings, and then was clear and still flying. His new name? Corregidor George.

There was old-time Navy man Ben Preston, fearless and belligerent, who lived for the next time he could throw a bomb at a Jap ship. He'd lead his planes through any obstacle just to give the Japs a chance to shoot at them while he and his boys knocked holy hell out of everything and anything that bore a Made-in-Japan label.

There were the fellows who never made it back, hard flying and eager with an overwhelming desire to sink Jap ships: Andy Rohleder, a wonderful, quiet boy, somebody's younger brother, but a cool and accurate pilot; Elmer Namoski, scrappy, chipper, with a wife at home; Wilson McNeil, like Namoski a married man, tall but soft-spoken, easygoing, always pleasant; and many others, all of whom left a well-marked trail behind them. A trail that started in the Palau Islands in the far Pacific; was marked by shot-down Jap planes, blasted Jap guns and bombed-out Jap ships; and, for each of these men, ended in the explosion of flame that a US Navy dive-bomber makes when it slams into a foreign ocean at 300 miles per hour with riddled wings and a flaming engine.

On the *Intrepid*, we of Bombing 18 had heard the legend of the mammoth Jap battleships and, like most of the Navy, we agreed that the only way to get rough with a battleship was with two other battleships. We said the only sane course to follow on sighting something like the *Yamato* was to execute that standard maneuver described as "doing a fast 180 degree turn and getting the hell out." We pictured ourselves zinging back to our fleet, nose down, tail over the shoulder, and from the US side of the battleline gesticulating madly as to the size and direction of the enemy battleships. It probably would have been the sane thing to do.

About the middle of October 1944, the pilots and crews of Bombing 18 were beginning to feel like veterans—and giving up all hope of returning alive. Shortly before, in the first strikes of Formosa, the squadron had been decimated. It seemed that most of the lieutenants in the squadron, along with the skipper, Lt. Comdr. Mark Eslick, Jr., had been killed.

Lt. Comdr. George Ghesquiere took over. He reorganized the squadron. Younger officers, the survivors, now led sections and divisions of planes.

A 1,000 pound message for Hirohito is carefully loaded into an Avenger's torpedo bay. USN via Intrepid Museum

VB–18's Helldivers prepare to launch. USN via Intrepid Museum

The general reshuffle and the new duties and responsibilities did much to revive the spark of the squadron and help the new flight leaders forget who had flown in those spots before them.

The evening of October 23 brought electrifying news: a sub near the Palawan in the far Philippines had sighted a tremendous Jap force headed toward us. The long-awaited battle of the fleets was in the making. The sub had launched a spread of torpedoes at a ship so large the captain might have mistaken it for an island. It was late in the day when we received the word. The sub contact was several hundred miles away, but it was clear to every man aboard that the next day would see the start of a climactic battle. The Second Battle of the Philippines had been joined.

On the fateful morning of October 24, we were dressed, fed and struggling into our flying gear long before dawn. The tension and the hum of nervous conversation in the ready room mounted steadily as pilots and crewmen checked their emergency rafts and gear, and recorded the ship's ever-changing position, the recognition signals and the codes to be used on their navigation plotting boards.

Messages from the bridge and air plot kept the speakers rasping and each announcement was greeted by a new wave of buzzing speculation. Four or five bombers were designated to fly a scouting hop to locate and bore sight the emperor's ships for the attack to follow. They roared down the deck and away into the predawn blackness. The rest of us crouched near the battle radio and thought our own thoughts or made small talk by betting which pilot would spot the enemy fleet, and how soon.

And then it came, just after daylight. Calm, imperturbable Max Adams broke radio silence, his message more exciting because of its clearness and

After launching, the Helldivers fly out in search of Japanese ships. USN via Intrepid Museum

the hint of strain that, so unlike Max, had crept into his voice. He gave his position—over the heart of the Jap-held Philippines—and then told what he saw: the heaviest sluggers of Japan, in battleline, swinging along straight for the San Bernardino Strait and our carriers and ships.

Then, the call to battle for every airman came, sharp and clear, over the squawker: "Pilots—man your planes." I hurried out onto the catwalk, along the edge of the flight deck and then aft along the deck. As I ducked around a big torpedo bomber I almost bumped into its pilot, tall Ray Skelly, a good-looking, well-liked southerner. Skelly looked grim and worried; I'd never seen him that way before.

I thought of the work cut out for him and his torpedo plane pilots, and was glad it wasn't me. I yelled, "You torpedoes are going to have it tough today."

In the tearing wind of the flight deck and his preoccupation Ray must have thought I said something else, because he said, "The hell you say, *we're* going to get it today!" And he did. He was killed that morning, shot down in flames in the central Philippines.

But now I climbed into the cockpit of my dive-bomber and minutes later, airborne and at an altitude of some 17,000 feet, we throbbed in over the rocky surf line and the lush green shore of southern Luzon in the Philippines. On we went toward the island of Panay and the hardly ruffled, sparkling water of the inland Sibuyan Sea.

It was a beautiful morning with a few big, fluffy white clouds and a crisp, bright cheerfulness in the air, so incongruous with our thick, blue-black Hellcats, Avengers and Helldivers, droning on in a tight formation, bristling with exposed machine guns and the long ugly nose fuses of wing bombs. We were twenty-six aircraft: twelve dive-bombers, ten torpedoes and four fighters.

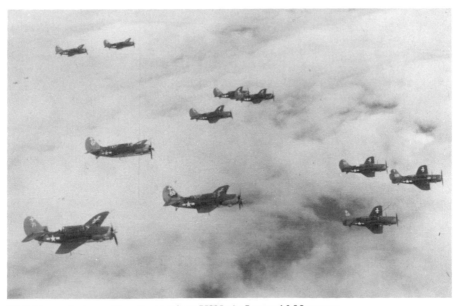

Helldivers in traveling formation. USN via Intrepid Museum

11

We had wanted more fighters but air combat patrols and fighter sweeps had drained them. Everyone wanted more fighters. A battleship admiral would have taken our last four except for our carrier admiral, who embarrassed him by offering the protection of the carrier's puny guns to the great floating fort of a battleship.

We wanted more bombers and torpedo planes too, but we were the first in the air and the closest, and we were ordered to hit with what we had.

Our training had taught us that eighteen planes to a ship was the desired ratio for a successful attack. Here we knew there were twenty-six planes against twenty-nine ships. The concentration of fire would be terrific. It was estimated that in that fleet there were more heavy flak guns concentrated in a slightly smaller area than in a certain deathtrap in the Ploesti Oil Fields, which an official publication has since said held the heaviest concentration of gunfire Allied airmen ever had to fly through. But with the freshness of the day and the sparkling sea, we were not bothered by statistics that morning.

Max Adams, in the scouting plane, had reported the enemy position as near the southeastern end of the Sibuyan Sea. As we droned on, halfway across the Philippines, the hills of Panay appeared and to their north the shimmering inland sea, wherein we knew the pride of the Japanese Navy was racing to the attack. The tension mounted and I found myself yawning one little nervous yawn after another. They were as uncontrollable as shivers.

The closer we got the more we could see. Eventually we could see the inland sea from the near shore to the horizon, all except the southeast corner, hidden from view by a huge roll of fluffy clouds ahead of and just below our flight path.

Where were those ships? Were they down behind that cloud? They must be. But were they? The suspense became maddening. I unconsciously

Helldivers coming in to the carrier. USN via Intrepid Museum

craned my neck to see over the edge of the clouds, and felt frustrated when my view was not increased.

The suspense became acute. At each second we expected to see the enemy. We could see almost all the water area and still no ships. My heart was thumping and still no ships. Then, we blasted over the edge of the fluffy clouds and the world changed as, with a black puff of AA fire, the Second Battle of the Philippines began for the *Intrepid*'s planes.

The sea ahead was alive with the boiling wakes of ships of the line and the churnings of their speedy escorts. The scene was lost to me because there, in the vanguard of the battlewagons, was the most fearsome thing I have ever beheld. It seemed that great letters of red and yellow fire exploded upward from that great hulk and burned into my mind. *YAMATO!*

As a small boy, reading fairy tales, I was impressed by nothing so much as the great dark castles of the bad ogres or giants that perched forebodingly atop the perpendicular walls of frowning cliffs. The heavy battlements presented the picture of deep, dangerous, evil power and absolute invincibility.

So was the picture of this ship to me. It dwarfed its sisters. Compared with them it seemed a fierce dark island dominated by the massive wall of its towering superstructure, which rose from aft of the immense turrets in a straight, unbroken line of hard, dark gray steel armor. It was the frowning, impenetrable fortress of the ogres.

I felt the hair on my neck rise. I knew to the bottom of my shoes that this would be my target. There was no assignment, no order, but there was no question. I had trained for this for three years; it was my duty, my job, my fate. I couldn't look away or at another ship. This held me in a fatal fascination, and it was oh, so real and oh, so fierce.

I awoke with a slam-banging start as AA burst so close I could hear its sharp report over the roar of the engine and howl of the slip-stream. I realized I'd been taking evasive action but now I yanked back on the stick and kicked rudder with all my 210 pounds, just as a whole series of AA bursts caught the dive-bomber. The bursts were so close I could hear them, some dull, many sharp, and others rattling and bouncing my tightly latched cockpit cover.

I slammed the controls back hard to the port. The stick and rudder kicked convulsively back against my hands and feet. I knew the plane was being hit, but I didn't have time to think how bad. I thought, *If it's so bad I can't dive, Brownie will tell me.* Brownie was Walter Brown, my eighteen-year-old, 120 pound gunner with a couple tons of guts and courage. But this was a silly thought. I'd know as quickly as he if the tail or a wing were blown off. I glanced up just in time to see both my wingmen—Ben Emge and Don Freet—flaring up and away. Emge told me later I was so covered with bursting flak that he pulled off rather than get shot down because he happened to know me.

I knew it was time to dive. I saw the skipper peel off in a sharp wingover and go straight down into the screaming vertical dive of the Navy dive-bombers. His wingmen followed in quick succession, black, white and red AA puffs marking their trail. My turn now, and I was in trouble. My plane was being bracketed steadily by explosions, and hit frequently by shrapnel. Ordinarily a dive was salvation, but now as I rolled over on my back and

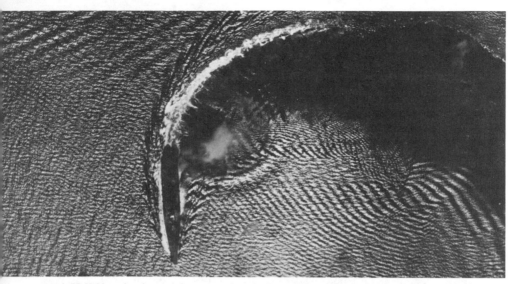

A Helldiver's view of the super battleship Musachi as the attack starts. USN

pulled the nose down toward the sea, I heard and felt more bursts; they still had my range.

I took violent evasive action. I twisted, corkscrewed and turned, things I'd never had to do in my dive before. My altimeter unreeled crazily as I spun and twisted straight down. At 6,000 feet I knew I had to stop all evasion and get on the target or I never would. My training took over. Forget the gunfire! I brought my ring sight down on that tremendous battlewagon. I stopped jinking and steadied my sight right on that turret. I looked death in the face.

The ship's decks were alive with gunfire. The bright orange-yellow flash-flash-flash of the multiple 5 or 6 inch batteries and the white almost continuous fire of the medium AA mixed in with streams of rising tracers from the smaller automatic cannons made it appear that we were diving into the exploding cauldron of hell itself.

I remember distinctly bore sighting the forward turret of that flame-spouting monster and then sitting back against the armor plate seatback of my Helldiver and relaxing. I'd done everything I could do. I knew I'd never get out alive; I couldn't be missed by all those shells. Yet I couldn't jink and get a hit, and more important than my life, I had to get a hit. I poised my whole hand over the thumb-button bomb release and prayed to myself that, as my last act, I'd be able to hit that release and send my 1,000 pound armor-piercing bomb slamming into the battleship's decks.

Having prepared myself and resigned myself, I became aware of the passage of time—2 or 3 seconds perhaps, but in a dive-bomber blasting straight down toward enemy decks, wide open, that's time. I knew I'd dived a long way, longer than I had a right to. I began to take heart.

A glance at the altimeter showed it whipping past 3,000 feet; time to drop that bomb and pull out. I brightened. Maybe I would get a chance to drop it, but not now. I was going to take that bomb down so low I couldn't miss. In my ring sight that huge number 2 turret was growing fast. It filled half the sight and then the whole sight; I was on top of it. I hit the bomb release, and yanked back the stick with all my might. I was hundreds of feet below minimum safe release altitude. Could I pull the plane out of that terrific full-throttle dive in the little altitude I had left with my flabby, shot-up controls?

I was doing it! As the nose came up, above the roar of that 2,000 horsepower engine and the shrieking wind of my wild dive I heard the crackle of the great battleship's lighter guns punctuated with the thumping blasts of her heavier AA. I saw tracers zip past my cockpit and watched holes appear as if my magic in my wings. Then with a zooming roar we cleared the water and shot 1,000 feet back into the air.

The g-force indicator showed 10½ g's pulled. At 210 pounds, my body had weighed over 1 ton at the height of pullout, but my heart bounced high when Brownie in the rear seat yelled into the intercom, "We got a hit, we got a hit, our bomb hit the ship right on her big back end!"

But there was more trouble. The best heavy cruisers of the Emperor's Navy were in line in front of me, and beyond them the destroyers lay between us and the open sea. Diving straight down into the middle of the Jap Navy was one thing, hedgehopping over them, one at a time, out to the edges, was another. Ahead of me a bucking, jinking dive-bomber was bolting for the open between two cruisers. The tracers from the ships formed an X with the bomber at the cross, every bullet seemed to pass through it yet it flew on.

I rolled my bomber flat on her back then pulled down and away in a great scooping rollout that carried me down to the surface and up and off in a sliding, skidding turn in the other direction. As I pulled through, I saw the torpedo planes, their attack perfectly timed—but what a job, low, close to the water, just zooming the guns of the enemy. The guts and courage to press home a torpedo attack go unexcelled in the annals of flying.

In a moment I was between the cruisers, the flashing of tracers making more holes in my wings. Then only the destroyers were ahead. What a relief to see the numbers and sizes of the ships getting smaller ahead. I braced my back against the armor plate behind me and put every ounce of my strength

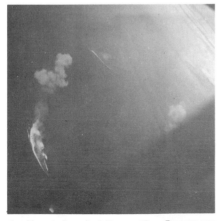

A direct bomb hit on the Japanese super battleship. USN via R. Shipman

Japanese battleship and cruiser. The black cloud on the right is bomb smoke from a direct hit on the stern of the ship. USN via Intrepid Museum

15

Large Japanese carrier, probably the Zuikaku, *dead in water and an* Ise-class *battleship. Severely damaged, the battleship abandons the sinking carrier.* USN

into the controls. I tried to make that 12,000 pounds of airplane a bouncing jackrabbit to the deadly serious machine gunners below.

In my wild maneuvers I glimpsed the great battlewagon, my target of a few moments before. From the smoke and flame of her guns she appeared almost on fire but I saw what I wanted. Against her sides rose high plumes of spray and smoke from hits by our bombs and torpedoes. Even in my backward glance a geyser of white water spouted higher than her masthead as a torpedo hit home.

I was well beyond the normal range one is shot at, yet still the black and red puffs followed—not so near now, but still right with me. I had had a glance at the water a few minutes ago. It had been placid but now it boiled and splashed. For a moment I couldn't comprehend. Then I realized: AA shells and fragments, some spent, some terrifyingly alive, were churning the surface as if the water was at full boil in a saucepan. I could hardly believe it. I looked again and jinked for my life.

In a minute more I was well clear and overcome with that feeling of buoyant relief and thanksgiving that only comes from being shot at, and being missed.

I saw no other airplanes. I felt like the only survivor; I didn't see how any plane could dive through that fire and come out. Then I saw other bombers and a few torpedo planes. Gradually they joined up until almost all were back in formation. It seemed incredible that so many could get through. True, they were holed and battered, but there they were. Don Freet and Ben Emge came back beside me. Ben's engine was smoking and cutting out for seconds every so often, but he worried it back across the Philippines and then out onto our haven, the broad Pacific, where American ships would find us if we went down into the water, and survived the crash. Miraculously, that tough Wright engine kept him in the air and brought him back to the ship.

16

The Musachi's sister ship under attack in 1945. The photo shows a miss to port, but a direct hit has been scored aft of her funnel. Attacks continued until she sank. Of the 3,000 men aboard, only 200 survived. USN

Lt. Wilson C. McNeill. A warm-hearted man who won deep affection and respect from the men who flew with him. He was killed over the Japanese fleet October 23, 1944. Lt. Donald Wilson

The wings of my own plane were riddled with holes and pieces were gone from the elevators and tail, but it flew and I blessed it. Later, aboard ship, it was declared unflyable and eventually pushed overboard to make way for the less-shot-up planes and the hectic operations of those next few days known as the Second Battle of the Philippines.

And what of that huge monster ship we'd struck? It was pounded all day by our Task Force 38.2 and at times during the day by strikes from other air groups of Task Force 38. Later we learned that the ship was really the *Musachi*, twin of the *Yamato*, and that the bombs and torpedos had done their work. She straggled. Then, late that night, in an orgy of fire and noise, she exploded and sank in the central Philippines.

That ship, the great effort of the Japanese to defeat our battlewagons, never saw our ships, and now lies battered and broken fathoms down as a tribute to the accuracy of Navy dive-bombing and to the skill and courage of our torpedo pilots.

Chapter 2

Philosophy

At the beginning of my Navy career, my philosophy about wartime flying was to learn, practice and work like hell, and all would go well. This was the "it won't happen to me," or the "I am indestructible," theory. Later, my philosophy was to work and fly as if all depended on me and pray as if all depended on God. I still couldn't comprehend "destruction," but I came to believe that I would never return home again. The odds seemed too great.

I'm not sure if the "old boys" ever felt that way. The ones I knew didn't pray.

Each squadron was sprinkled with old boys. They were combat-hardened lieutenants, men who'd joined the Navy before Pearl Harbor and who'd fought at Midway, the Coral Sea and many other places. They were survivors and they lived by a tough code.

Ben Preston and Leif Larson were examples. Their approach to the war was "Let's win it. Go all out, get a hit, do the maximum possible damage at each hop. Be aggressive as hell but not careless or reckless. Get back to the ship so you can go bomb them again tomorrow." They would have agreed with Tom Wolfe, as he wrote in *The Right Stuff:* "Anyone could throw his life away needlessly but that was not the right stuff."

Preston and Larson wanted their lives to count, even though they laid them on the line each day, and wanted to. Curiously, the old boys were in the lowest casualty group. More of them would survive in the coming months than of any other group within the squadron.

The squadron was also sprinkled with lieutenants who had been instructors. They were in the squadron because they had requested fleet duty. They became the group with the highest casualties—fifty percent. Every other one of them didn't make it home.

The contrasts between and within the two groups gradually became evident. The full lieutenants who had been instructors had had to teach safety. For some this had become and remained an important part of flying.

Safety, as such, was not a part of Preston's or Larson's thinking. I know, I felt a rule about safety or safe practices was an invitation to see how far it could be violated. You either proved the rule silly or, at some extreme violation of the rule, scared the hell out of yourself and decided that was about as far as you ought to go—this time.

Lt. Wilson "Mac" McNeil, as an instructor, must have been patient, encouraging and thorough. He was an excellent pilot. Everyone liked him. He was quiet, polite, but had a fine sense of humor. He was just a great

An echelon of Helldivers. USN via R. F. Dorr

person. While instructing, he had requested sea duty. The request was granted and he was ordered to VB–18. He led a division of six Helldivers and he led them against the Japanese fleet in the Second Battle of the Philippines.

At our first contact in that battle, on October 24, 1944, the Japanese fleet was storming along through the central Philippines heading for San Bernardino Strait to breakout and to meet our fleet head-on. It was their big push to smash our fleet, and although we had power, they had plenty of strong cards and intended to play them well, as they had when they rolled over the countries and outposts in the far Pacific at the start of the war.

Mac McNeil was on the second strike from the *Intrepid.* I'd been on the earlier strike. As my flight had neared the ships the entire Jap fleet had opened up with antiaircraft fire—bursts everywhere, whole clouds of bursts. Our only defenses at that point were to throw out chaff to confuse their radar and to take maximum evasive action.

In the stateside world there are two levels of maximum possible evasive action. The first level is limited by trying not to jink so hard that your cadet-in-training wingman can't stay with you. The second level is limited by safety—no midairs, please.

But out over the Pacific, when the antiaircraft comes whamming in, there is only one level of maximum possible evasive action and that is an all-out, no-holds-barred level—the hell with the wingman, the hell with safety. Make that airplane jump!

That October morning I put my entire weight into working those controls in a truly violent manner and the plane responded. I was all over the sky. My wingmen? Ben Emge and Don Freet stayed in there with me. I knew they would. In training we had practiced unauthorized, wild tail chases across the sky, and they proved that if I could do it they could do it and they stayed alongside.

As Mac approached the Jap fleet, the antiaircraft fire was again all-pervasive. It came in bursts of red, black, brown, purple and white. Each

19

ship must have had its own color so the spotters on board could identify their own bursts and then could correct the aim for the ship.

The white bursts were the most alarming. They were exploding white phosphorus shells. After the initial bursts, white streamers flew outward in all directions. At the head of each streamer was a blazing chunk of phosphorus. Phosphorus burns so hot it will burn right through a wing, a fuselage or a pilot. You had the same desire to avoid it that you would have to avoid a rattlesnake trying to get into your cockpit.

Right over their ships, the Japs had concentrated their white phosphorus shells until there was a whole cloud of white phosphorus smoke with constant lightninglike flickers and flashes as more shells burst in it. I had watched as one dive-bomber after another pushed over and went straight down, right through that exploding cloud.

Mac could see all this, and even though I wasn't there, I know he was taking maximum possible evasive action, but which kind? The stateside training and safety form, or the Pacific life or death form? Regardless, they shot his plane apart and he died in it.

I'll always wonder, if Mac hadn't been required to teach safety so long or hadn't had to make allowances for his wingmen-in-training for so long, would he have jinked even harder and maybe survived that barrage?

Among the ex-instructors was another group of pilots so anxious to get out of instructing and to fight the war that they would take any risk, the bigger the better—the hell with the odds, man, fight the war.

Walt Madden and Elmer "Nemo" Namoski were of this caliber. They had in common their aggressiveness, their disregard of the odds against them and the desire to contribute significantly to victory.

Madden traded his life to burn a fully loaded Japanese oil tanker and even today, from his heavenly seat, I'll bet he looks back with pride at finding the ship, splitting from the squadron and sinking that ship.

Members of VB–18 in Hilo, Hawaii, 1944, waiting for the action to start. Left to right: Ensigns Jim Chaney, Morris Anderson and Al Ehrke; Lts. Walter Madden and Elmer Namoski; Ensign Jack Linn. Lt. V. M. Serrell

At 5 feet 10 inches, Nemo was not tall but he was quick and tough. He was a boxer in college and good enough to have made a career of it if he had wanted to. Typically, he would challenge anyone to put on the gloves with him or, if his opponents preferred, to go a few rounds without gloves.

I was 6 feet 3 inches and yet every so often, when we had a good drinking party going, Nemo would come over and ask me to step outside and fight, for no other reason than that he wanted to take on a big guy. He was serious and, since he was good at boxing, he probably could have handed me trouble.

Besides that, I had another rule of my father's in mind. If you are a big guy, don't get in a fight with a small guy. You'll look bad if you lose, and you'll look bad if you win. You're suspected of picking on the little guy. So I would laugh him off and hand him another drink. The drinks were a quarter. It seemed like a good investment.

Nemo was a full lieutenant and this was his first combat duty. On October 29, 1944, we bombed Clark Field, north of Manila. It was the largest, most important air base in the Philippines, built by Americans for Americans, but now used by the Japanese.

We found Jap fighters airborne and Jap fighters taking off as we arrived.

Nemo and his division executed their dive-bombing runs with professionalism. The damage was maximum. But then, as he pulled out of his dive, right ahead of him but still on the ground was a Jap fighter making his takeoff run.

An airplane taking off is a sitting duck for attack from the air. He can't maneuver until he's airborne, but you'd better not miss because if you overfly him, he's on your tail and that's deadly.

Every pilot, especially a bomber pilot, wants to shoot down another plane, particularly a fighter. Add to that Nemo's aggressiveness and his desire to take on the big guys, along with his total disregard of the odds against him and his intense will to help win the war, and you have an irresistible situation.

Nemo had cast the die and it would be him or his enemy. As he came out of the dive-bombing run, he had the two best things one plane could have over another: speed and altitude. I wasn't in his cockpit but I know what happened. Nemo put his sights on the fighter's nose and fired a burst, but the range was too great. He could see the bullets hit and explode down the runway behind the fighter.

As the fighter became airborne, Nemo aimed again, but because of the angle of the dive and the gross difference in speed, if he brought his nose up enough to hit the target it obscured the target.

He pulled the nose up anyway, estimated his point of aim and fired a long burst. The ground was coming up fast. He pulled back on the stick and zoomed over the fighter, up and away. But not really away. He'd missed the fighter and by this time the fighter was not only airborne but was building up the speed he needed to attack. As Nemo passed over his head, the fighter pilot pulled his agile plane up on its tail and pulled the trigger. The fighter's cannons and machine guns tore into the belly of the dive-bomber, ripped through the fuselage and into the engine, smashed the controls, and smashed hydraulic and gasoline lines. The entire bottom of the Helldiver burst into flames.

The Helldiver was a sturdy plane that could take great punishment and return again to fight, but this was too much. With the controls shot out and flames everywhere, Elmer Namoski's connections to this life came apart. He died in the crash near Clark Field. His gunner, Sterling E. Graham, was able to parachute from the flaming plane, but he no sooner hit the ground than he was machine-gunned to death by the Japanese garrison at the little Philippine community of Conception.

What was the best philosophy for this work? Perhaps a cross between sanity and utter disregard for the odds against you. I could summarize by saying, "Fly crazy but be smart."

Victor E. "Tim" Serrell had a workable program. He had graduated from Cornell with an engineering degree. He didn't want a war and he didn't want to be in it, but since there was a war and he was in it, like Preston and Larson, he would do all possible to maximize his effectiveness and his chances of returning home.

Serrell organized us all to strafe more effectively. He brought us recognition photos of enemy shipping with the vital part of each type circled in red. He asked us all to identify the type of ship in our sights and then to concentrate our fire on its vitals.

To assist the Lord in bringing him home, he went to the parachute loft and had the chief sew short lengths of light rope on his flight coveralls—around his arms at the elbows and the shoulders, and around his legs below the knee and at his upper thigh. The ropes were twisted so a pull on the end would tighten and bind them around his arm or leg as a tourniquet.

Serrell had seen how difficult it was for a wounded man in a small cockpit to apply a tourniquet and philosophized that a stitch in time saves those who take it. All he had to do was pull on the appropriate cord and the blood would be cut off. Irreverently, we suggested that he sew one more rope on his flight suit, around his neck. We laughed at the homemade tourniquet idea, but—maybe—?

Much of anyone's philosophy comes from one's family. My father, Ben Forsyth, had been a hockey star. He had also played football for his high school, his prep school, two universities and an all-star service team.

While in college he was paid to race motorcycles. He became a private in the US Army Cavalry and later, after he had come home, received a second lieutenant's commission in the Cavalry. In the meantime World War I had started and he had joined the Navy as an enlisted man, and later he became a seagoing officer in the Navy.

He was a woodsman, a hunter and a fisherman. Most of his life, he was a trial lawyer. He lived where the action was. He spent a great deal of time with his three sons, and we learned our philosophies from his stories and his conduct. Life was adventure and action, and for me, US Navy carrier flying was where it was.

When at age twenty-one I left to go to war, I had what he'd taught me about manly things. I didn't think there was much he could add in our last hour before I left, but he did. "Jack," he said, "I have just one request. It's from your mother and me. Do your best and do your duty but don't volunteer for hazardous extra duty."

He must have thought about that a great deal beforehand and I know I thought about it as much afterwards. It was a lasting guide, a standard by which to judge things, a bit of sanity and balance that I surely needed.

Thoughts on philosophy and volunteers would not be complete without comment on the Japanese Kamikazi Corps, the suicide corps. As the most experienced Japanese pilots and their best planes were ground up in combat, the situation became desperate and the Japanese called for volunteers to strike a blow for glory and country by deliberately crashing their planes into our ships.

The young Japanese responded in unbelievable numbers to give their lives for their country. They rode to their deaths in sleek fighters or rickety obsolete aircraft. They rode in flying bombs and as human torpedos. They took a tremendous toll of our ships but our military-industrial complex, with the help of all our citizens, had supplied us with so much overpowering equipment that we won anyway.

The question often thought but never discussed was, Would our young men have done the same? If our country were in desperate straits and suicide squadrons appeared to be the only answer to invasion, destruction and enslavement, would our men have joined such squadrons? I have to think the answer is yes.

The other question is: If third world or other countries would ask or allow their best young people to intentionally sacrifice their lives for their country would not that country first use every weapon it had, including poison gas and atomic bombs. Again I have to think the answer is yes.

Perhaps the concept of unconditional surrender should be discarded and replaced with the concept of negotiated settlements, of fighting wars so as not to press a country so hard that it would pull the nuclear trigger and end the world.

A medium carrier (CVL) and her big brothers. USN via R. F. Dorr

Chapter 3

In the beginning

In September 1939, German armies, at the command of Adolf Hitler, invaded Poland and the world, whether it knew it then or not, was at war. Americans had difficulty accepting the concept that a war was on and that we would be involved. Doves, called isolationists, were everywhere.

Here and there were people who could look at unpleasant, difficult situations and evaluate them with relative objectivity. In their opinion, no matter how much we deplored what was going on, we could not let our feelings keep us from seeing that Hitler must be opposed strongly or capitulated to. Force would be used against us and the only response that could contain such a person was, like it or not, force.

Other people, blinded by nationalism or naiveté, believed America was up-to-date and strong militarily, and no greater defense effort was necessary.

The objective people knew that America had already passed the time when it should be arming and training itself. They knew we had no forces to match the weapons, manpower and training of the German armies. They subtly urged preparedness on us, couching their language in terms of "defense."

Fortunately, the realists among us had been able to take some basic steps toward the preservation of our world. In early 1939, the US government had initiated the Civilian Pilot Training (CPT) Program. President Franklin Roosevelt announced from his fireside that the future belonged to the air-minded, that everyone would be flying and that we needed pilots. He labeled it a civilian program to mollify the public but it was a vital war measure.

Later, after Pearl Harbor, he stunned us all by the magnitude of his projections of what our military-industrial complex would build for us in tanks and ships and planes. "My friends," he said, "we shall train 36,000 men and women to fly. We will train more pilots than now exist in the Army, Navy and Airlines combined."

He was right, because the CPT Program had, for two years, been supplying Americans with a cadre of pilots who would now train the pilots we needed for the war.

I graduated from high school in June 1939 and had been accepted to attend the University of Rochester in the fall. I had heard of the CPT Program. I joined it and learned to fly that summer. Pretty heady stuff.

I've always liked and run engines. I thrive on the surge of power from engines, from a small outboard to a big new V–8 in a sports car. To me, the sound of an engine starting is an audio security blanket. I love the sound and the responsiveness.

I've also sailed all my life, particularly in light, sensitive craft where you can feel every nuance of the wind—its direction, its weight and its effect on the airfoil, the sail. When my two loves—engines and sails—combine, synergism creates the ultimate: a powerful, sensitive aircraft.

So there I was, July 14, 1939, sitting in a 65 horsepower Taylor-Craft, just off the end of runway 22 at Rochester, New York, with the chief instructor, Pete Barton. We were waiting for a flash of green light from the tower so I could take off. This was to be my last dual ride before I soloed. I was nervous but not half as nervous as the pilot of another small plane in the air approaching the end of the runway for a landing.

It was a yellow Piper Cub and it was flying erratically—first too high, then too low, then in a jerky overcontrol to the left, then back on track but high. It came over the runway 25 feet in the air and landed there, 25 feet over the pavement. Of course, it didn't stay there for long—it immediately dropped to the ground, causing the landing gear shock cords to part and the wheels to bounce up and pierce the wings. The propeller came out as a shattered stub and gasoline started running out on the runway. The pilot, perceiving his errors and mindful of the gasoline, also bounced out and started running. The whole procedure precipitated other action, namely the arrival of two fire trucks, an ambulance and a much-annoyed head of the flying school, who was the owner of the plane.

All this was about as much as I could take one flight hour before I was to solo. I waited for a better time.

My day for solo came. My regular instructor, Milt Carsdale, and I flew around the pattern. Then we stopped and he climbed out and said, "Take her around the field, she's yours."

I wasn't sure I wanted her. My hands were sweaty and I'm sure my heartbeat was elevated. I didn't particularly trust that instructor anyway and I wasn't sure I believed him when he said I was ready. However, it was sink or swim in the flying game, so I took my courage in my own two hands and taxied off to the takeoff spot.

I'd had 8 hours of flying in that cockpit but now, as I sat at the takeoff spot, everything looked a little foreign and dangerous. I handled the controls gingerly, half expecting some unexpected effect when I moved them. I'd been looking for adventure and excitement—well, this was it, enjoy it fellow. But, as with so many thrills, I would enjoy this one most after it was completed.

I carefully opened the throttle about halfway and sure enough the plane gathered speed. I knew I needed full throttle and kept pushing it forward, but most respectfully. Finally, I had full power and was just getting used to it when the sensitive little plane began flying—it just came off the ground like that and I was airborne. It was exhilarating. The ground was dropping away from me and the controls were firm, their response controlled and normal. I heaved a big sigh and realized I had hardly been breathing as I took off. I looked at the empty seat beside me and had that wonderful glow of pride and excitement that makes it all worthwhile.

Now all I had to do was fly a pattern around the field, find the other end of the runway and get down low enough so I could land—land on the ground, not 25 feet in the air. I almost froze. Suppose I did stall out at 25 feet, as that Cub had done yesterday?

The picture in my mind of that little disaster dominated my thoughts and about ruined my coordination. I came toward the landing end of the runway, reduced my throttle and tried to follow a reasonable glide to the runway. I came over the edge of the field at about the right height but fifty percent faster than I should be—I was making sure I wouldn't stall in. The speed compounded my problem. As I eased back on the stick to level out I ballooned back into the air. I almost panicked—now I was high and slow. I had to put the stick ahead. I did and the airplane started to drop with a sickening lurch.

If I had held the stick steady the little plane would have settled graciously back to earth for a good landing, but when I pushed the stick ahead it started down in a hurry, helped by the control and gravity. Next the plane was porpoising and I was truly alarmed. I could have hit the throttle and gone up and around again, but would I have been too late and too slow and stalled anyway? My other alternative was to lock that stick in my hands and not let myself jerk it back and forth as I tried to level out at the ground level. I couldn't stop pulling the stick; my reflexes were too strong. I was holding it in my right hand, so I jammed my right elbow into my gut and held it there. With that elbow locked against me I couldn't pull back too far. With the stick steady and firm the oscillation ceased and the great little plane just about landed itself. I rolled to a stop and wiped off the bead of sweat. I'd soloed. My life would never be the same again.

The Civilian Pilot Training Program started with a Primary course, in which you learned to fly in 65 horsepower Cubs, soloed and learned basic navigation, power plants, theory of flight, weather, air traffic rules, stalls and spins, and a variety of nonaerobatic flying maneuvers like Eights Around a Pylon. It was a great summer.

The next CPT course was Secondary. It was taught in open-cockpit biplanes with helmets, goggles and parachutes. It consisted of aerobatics and exercises such as Eights On a Pylon and Cuban Eights.

Eights Around are easy, Eights On are frustrating, Cuban Eights are fun. In Eights Around you select two points (say, trees) on the ground and fly figure eights around them, keeping equally distant from the points at all times.

In Eights On you select two pylons located so that a line between them is at right angles to the wind direction. You then fly eights around these pylons but this time you try to keep your wing tip pointed right at the pylons. The effect of the wind causes you to continuously increase your bank as you go around the pylons. It is a neat exercise in coordination and perception.

In Cuban Eights you fly an eight lying on its side in the vertical plane. You start as though making a loop, but after you go over the top and your nose is 45 degrees down on the other side, you roll upright and start the other half of the eight, again as though starting a loop. This is disorienting, since you are changing direction and altitude and from upright to inverted to upright in quick succession, but it is fun when you're flying smoothly with reference to the horizon—even though the horizon may be overhead, under the plane or spinning off to one side.

The CPT Program was well worked out. The instructors wanted you to learn to do all your airplane could do. The program was big on stalls, spins and rolls, including slow, snap and aileron rolls. This hard work in basic flying skills proved unbelievably useful to me later on when flying dive-bombers and fighters in violent maneuvers.

In CPT we did spins almost every day until they were precise, controlled maneuvers. One instructor, for excitement, occasionally did a twenty-five or thirty-turn spin straight down. I would have been too dizzy to pull out. One day in September, over a local carnival, to thrill the crowd, he started a spin at only 300 feet above the ground. He miscalculated; he needed 350 feet. That was the first fatality among my friends.

The third CPT course was Cross-Country Flying in a Stinson Reliant, which was a five-place, luxury plane that cruised at 125 miles per hour. It had a control wheel instead of a stick, leather seats and even ashtrays. We thought it was super.

The fourth course was Instruments and was a problem for me. My reactions to my own senses were too strong for me to rely on my instruments; I would have a touch of vertigo at the drop of a wing tip. I worked hard to pass the course but it was always scary.

One night, near the city of Utica, New York, I dropped a pencil on the cabin floor. Both the instructor and I reached for it. I retrieved it in 5 or 10 seconds and looked up. I saw a row of lights that could have been a row of street lights from the town except that they were moving smartly across my windshield from top to bottom. For a long second I couldn't figure that one out.

Thankfully, comprehension comes quickly in tense situations, but no matter how quickly it comes, a little shock of fright comes first, wracks you and then stays with you for a while, even after you understand what is happening to you and realize it is not a major emergency. In this case, during our few seconds of inattention and undoubtedly by my unconsciously pulling the wheel to the right as I reached down to pick up the pencil, the plane had gone into a steep right turn. Thus, the street lights that should have been level appeared to pass from the top to the bottom of the windshield. It was a dangerous situation only if I didn't take proper remedial action. We recovered from the turn immediately but to this day I'm very careful about how I reach for anything that drops to the floor, in any moving vehicle.

There was one more CPT course, Instructing. On completion of that I had my commercial, instructor's and instrument ratings and had just finished my sophomore year in college to boot.

It was summer again. I was asked to instruct new students in Primary and was pleased to do so. By midterms, I was elevated to Secondary to teach aerobatics in the open biplane—helmet, goggles, flight suit and all. We Secondary instructors were hot stuff on the field and loved it.

We certainly weren't goof-proof, though. One instructor forgot to buckle his 6 inch wide, triple-snap safety belt. Later, in the air, he instructed his student to perform a slow roll. This instructor was the relaxed type and was calm and easy as the roll began. As the plane approached the inverted, my friend had the sensation that things were a little too loose and relaxed and glanced down just in time to see both ends of his safety belt hanging straight out from their bases, completely unfastened. His reactions were quick—if they hadn't been, he'd been riding as test pilot for a parachute that probably had never been used before. He stuck out both his elbows, and they caught where the lips of the cockpit sloped inward. There he hung until the roll was completed. He was still casual but not nearly so much so.

Occasionally, especially in learning to do spins, a Primary student would be actively airsick. This was harder on the instructor than the student. In the Taylor-Craft trainer, the student sat in front of the instructor, and when he let go, the instructor received most of it. We were thus encouraged to monitor our students' feelings closely, and should there be any signs of airsickness, to fly straight and level to let them recover. The Taylor-Craft trainer had a fore and aft sliding window. If a student became ill, I'd make him stick his whole head out the window, then I'd push the sliding window closed against his neck and let him york. The slip-stream still blew some of it back in but it was a big improvement even if a little barbaric.

The Secondary program covered every aerobatic maneuver except an outside loop. It included such esoteric flying activities as the Falling Leaf, the Vertical Reverse and the Hesitation Roll. We did not call them stunts. They were aerobatics. The aerobatics were the ultimate instruction on how an airplane flies and how to control it in weird positions.

It was easy to imagine that you were flying your biplane against the World War I flying aces of the Red Baron Squadron or, with a bit more imagination, that you were in a new Hellcat stalking Zeros in the far Pacific. The more we imagined, the more we wanted the real thing, and this led to impatience, and with me, a search for more adventure and excitement than even the aerobatics provided.

An early manifestation was my delight in flying upside-down. I discovered that because of the shape of the airfoil, the aircraft would lose altitude faster inverted than upright. Our instruction took place near the field at a fairly high altitude. To lose altitude, quickly, at the end of the lesson, I'd fly home inverted, rolling out just before final approach.

Flying inverted in an open cockpit is a different sensation. You no longer seem to be enclosed in the security of an airplane. When you roll over and look around, it really hits you that there is nothing between you and the ground but air. It gives me a spooky jolt no matter how many times I've done it.

I was constantly on the lookout for new excitement. Playing in cloud canyons was a joy. You could duck in, out and around those fluffy white, billowing walls. You could climb, dive or twist through the clear lanes between the canyon sides. It was beautiful and exciting beyond words. It was a three-dimensional lark in fairyland. You had the freedom to turn in any direction or to go up or down and around as you willed. You shed the bounds and limits of earth and gravity. It was like riding Pegasus to adventure and beauty. I long to do it again.

One day when I was looking for "more," I discovered a thrill that never became tame. I had noticed a farm field below our aerobatic practice area in which grew two beautiful old elm trees. Elms have long trunks, clear of branches; their branches start high on the trunks and spread upward and outward. They are magnificent trees. These two grew near enough to each other so that 50 or 60 feet above the ground their branches almost touched, but no branches grew out sideways at the lower levels. The space between the trunks and branches was shaped like a church window, an arch. As I flew by, I wondered, Could an airplane fly through that arch?

For three days, I flew past those trees and wondered. The fourth day, I tried it. I brought the Waco biplane down to fence-top level and headed for the trees. The closer I came, the smaller the arch looked. It took all my nerve, supported by my prior estimates of size, to keep going. At the last second, if I hadn't been so scared, I'd have closed my eyes, but zip and I was through it without touching a leaf.

Now I had something that nobody else had and I let my students share the experience one by one. I'm sure none of them enjoyed it, but it had to be educational. I really don't believe the talk that two of them quit flying because of those trees.

Chapter 4

Welcome to the flying Navy

Pearl Harbor was devastated December 7, 1941. I knew I would have to go; the question was when and how. By the spring of 1942, I had a plan worked out. I would attend college all summer on the school's accelerated course, which meant I could graduate in January rather than waiting until the following June. This also meant I could complete the fall term before going into the service, my incentive being that I could play football one more season before leaving college for good.

Like almost everyone else at the time, I wanted to serve where the action was, and I decided to join as an aviation cadet, so I could have fleet duty. I was concerned that because of my civilian flying experience, they might make me an instructor for life. Here again my father's good counsel came in.

Dad had been an officer and enlisted man in both the Army and the Navy and said, "Join the Navy. You may be killed as quickly one place or the other but in the meantime, in the Navy, you'll have clean bedding, clean clothes, plentiful food and mud-free living quarters."

I objected, "But I want to fly with the fleet and only cadets get combat duty."

Dad came back, "Jack, as an officer, you will have a much better chance of obtaining the duty you want than as a cadet, believe me."

I followed his advice and it worked, and I was flying service-type aircraft 1½ years sooner than if I'd gone in as a cadet.

I attended college all the summer of 1942, and at the same time, I instructed in the pilot training programs at the local airport. Later in the year the students were all Army and Navy cadets in the preflight program.

By midsummer I was getting restless to enter the Navy and get on with the real flying and the war. I was assured I could join immediately as an officer and receive orders to active duty on whatever date I chose.

I had to time this carefully. Football was over in early November, but the fall term didn't end until January. If I stayed until late November, then, deducting Christmas vacation, there would be only a little over a month of the term left and I gambled that they would give me my degree even if I didn't stay for final exams. I tried this plan and it worked.

The only close call came with the chemistry professor. I wasn't doing well at all in chemistry, and he felt that if I'd take a special exam, he might have more on which to judge me and could give me a better grade. I didn't want him judging me any further—I knew I didn't know my chemistry and I didn't want him to find out how bad I really was in his favorite subject.

In any event, we set a date for the exam and I made sure it was as late as possible. It was to be the day before I was to leave. I'd been sworn in. I had my uniform. I put on my Navy blues with the gold stripe and went to his office. The sight of me in my uniform, ready to leave, flustered him for a moment and then he said, "Well maybe it really isn't necessary to take the exam." I agreed with him quickly, shook his hand and left. I thus jumped the final hurdle to the bestowal of a degree in absentia, and without taking final exams.

I had Thanksgiving dinner at home, at noon, then said good-bye to my brothers and father, hugged and kissed my mom, and took the train for New York City. I had my active-duty physical the next morning.

I flunked the physical. My blood pressure was off the scale. The corpsman said, "Go out and take a walk, sir. Calm down and come back and we'll see what happens." I took the walk, had a bowl of cream of tomato soup at the Chock-Full-O-Nuts store, went back and passed the exam.

Now, as planned, I had the weekend free, and, also as planned, I took a train to Providence, Rhode Island, and Brown University, where a special young lady was attending Pembroke College. She was tall and slender. She had long curly brown hair; it was sort of feather-cut and framed her face beautifully. We spent two great days together—and I do mean days, not nights. That's the way it was done then, darn it!

I arrived at Pensacola, Florida, late in the evening a few days later. I was liking Navy life already. Everyone greeted me with a snappy salute, treated me with respect and said sir. They had a neat officers club with twenty-five-cent drinks and good food. Everyone was in the war to win and they were purposeful and serious, and so was I.

At 5:00 a.m. after the first night I spent at Pensacola, I awoke to an earsplitting roar, as if all the airplane engines in the world had been started right outside my window.

That was reveille in Pensacola. It was the end of sleep. You couldn't even talk to your roommate with all the noise. So up and out to breakfast, and then to the administration building to report in.

I rounded the corner of the building and had my first look at Navy flying in action. An SNJ trainer was apparently having an emergency of some kind. The pilot was obviously trying to land but he was in terrible position to do so. He was just off the end of the runway but heading at right angles to it. He was making a sharp, low-altitude turn to try to line up and come over the runway. As an instructor, I shuddered. If he wasn't extremely skillful, he'd never get out of this one. But he did. He continued the sharp turn until just before the plane dropped the last 5 feet to the ground, when he rolled it level, made a smooth three-point landing and taxied off on the first taxiway.

I breathed a sigh of relief and looked back—and there was another SNJ in trouble, doing the same thing, and another and another. One after another, all the planes that came in followed this crazy and, I thought, dangerous pattern. It went on all day, as this was the basic pattern for an approach to a carrier. Of course, I learned to do it too, and with gusto!

At Pensacola I was part of a class of brand-new officers, but only two of us, Louis Swick and I, were flyers. We spent the first thirty days learning to be Naval officers. We took courses that introduced us to seamanship, anchoring and some basic weapons. We drilled, studied Naval regulations and took instruction in Naval customs and courtesy.

After that, Louis and I were sent to an outlying airfield to take the Navy's primary course. We were to fly Stearman biplanes. The N2S was the Navy's designation for this aircraft; the Yellow Peril was ours.

We arrived by bus and piled out to look and wonder at the show. Swarms of yellow biplanes were taking off and landing and coming and going like bees. Slowly we could discern a pattern; a flow at the takeoff area; a flow as they departed; another flow pouring in from another direction, toward the field; and a flow to the landing pad.

There were no radios or other control from the field. How did they make it work? The answer seemed to be specific instruction, discipline and fear of being washed out.

Louis and I were issued flight gear, real Navy stuff: helmets, goggles, long white silk scarfs, cloth summer jackets and coveralls, real leather jackets with mouton fur collars and light, pliable, smooth leather flying gauntlets, which would protect your hands from fire or flash burn, yet were so soft and pliable that you could pick up a pin.

We were given the field regulations manual to study and could hardly believe the instructions. Page 3 dealt with slipping an aircraft. Slipping is a useful way to lose altitude quickly when you're too high to land where you want. It's a little hazardous because you are coming in slowly, with your engine idling; you are getting near the ground; and you have to cross your controls to make it slip.

In CPT training, we would never allow a student to slip below 100 feet from the ground, but here the main safety regulation stated, "No pilot will slip an aircraft closer than five feet from the ground." We experienced that little flutter of excitement and laughed out loud.

Another section of the regulations was explicit on what is to be done if fog obliterates the field and you're still up. In civilian life, air controllers and airborne pilots from all over would pitch in to help you find a clear field or escort you down.

The Navy instructions were, "Climb north (away from the Gulf of Mexico) until you run out of gas and then bail out." Yikes! We wouldn't have dared bail out of one of Ray Hyland's trainers in Rochester. He'd have been furious. We used to say that instead of a parachute, he'd put cut-up newspapers in our parachute packs just so we would never jump out of one of his planes. Planes were hard to come by in civilian flying.

The Navy expected us to jump out of one of its Yellow Perils? If we flew north and jumped, we'd land in the Okefenokee or Tombigbee swamps. Now there would be an adventure!

Flying the primary program wasn't hard but it wasn't stress free either. Louis and I had flown enough so we didn't have to worry about "busting out," as the cadets did, but we certainly were learning new things about airplanes and new procedures. The Navy wanted its pilots to know basic flying before anything else. A Stearman trainer was a basic airplane—two wings and a motor, no flaps, spoilers or other flying aids or crutches. You started with this, and after you could take off and land it, the Navy-type fun began in the form of a pattern called S-Turns to a Circle.

The circle was a 50 foot diameter circle marked on the ground in the middle of an airfield. The theory was that any time after you'd taken off and started a circular pattern around the field, if your engine quit, you should still be able to glide to a landing and time your glide adequately enough to land within a 50 foot circle at the center of the field.

You'd be flying in the pattern, and when the instructor felt you were least expecting it or were out of position, he could chop the throttle. If he cut the engine when you were near the upwind edge of the field you had to turn downwind quickly, and on the downwind side you had to bank steeply near the ground and close to the circle to reach the circle.

If you were nearly downwind when he chopped the throttle you had to burn up altitude or else overfly the circle. You did this by making an S-turn. As you approached the field, you flew to the right of the straight-in glide path, then flew to the left of the runway. When you'd used up just the right amount of altitude, you flew right again. At the last minute, you turned to the runway heading upwind and dropped in, hopefully on the circle. Remember, when you're low, slow and gliding without power, 50 feet is a small target. Hitting it required skill, judgment and constant correction of course.

Eventually, we thoroughly enjoyed the procedure and it was a fabulous test of flying skills. Louis and I found little ways to extend or shorten a glide that could be done if your plane was stressed for it. The Stearman was built to military specifications and was rugged.

If it looked as though I would be short of the circle, I would come in high and stall the plane perhaps 30 feet in the air. The plane's momentum, even though stalled, would carry it another 40 or 50 feet toward the circle and I might hit it. I had to learn to ignore the shuddering crash with which the Stearman landed. If I was going to be long and overfly the circle, I stayed high and slow. Then at the right point, I dove for the deck, and just before I flew into the ground, I whipped back the stick, snap stalling the plane 5 feet over the ground. The snap separated the airflow from the wing, and the plane was through flying and hopefully on the ground in the circle.

This type of flying was hard on the instructors who didn't know whether you were an experienced pilot performing a controlled maneuver or a raw cadet crashing. Most instructors had the word quickly and a couple even asked us to show them some of the rolls and snaps the Navy didn't teach.

I'm afraid, though, that at times I caused problems at the field. For instance, there was no traffic control of any kind at the field with the circle on it. The air was full of Yellow Perils, all trying to hit the spot without hitting another plane. When three or four planes were trying to land on the circle at almost the same time, some of the pilots would have to put on the power and go around. The ones who made it were either the bravest or the stupidest of the pilots in the melee.

We all tried to be a little considerate, but the meaning of "a little considerate" varies from man to man, and on at least one occasion an instructor didn't believe I was being "a little considerate" enough.

I don't know what happened to incur this officer's ire. I was concentrating on getting to the circle like everybody else but must have pushed a little close to the instructor and made him go around. I don't blame him for being cautious; he might have been jousting with a cadet who really didn't have all that much control in jockeying for position.

As it was, I was solo, I'd competed for the landing spot, made the landing, bounced into the air, added full throttle and in 3 minutes was back up in the pattern coming downwind about to make a turn to start another S-Turn to the Circle. I glanced over my right shoulder to be sure I was clear to make my turn, but I wasn't. Six feet away was another Stearman right smack on my wing. There was no way I could turn. I was startled to see the plane there and startled again to see the instructor pilot who was glaring at me from the front cockpit. He was a chunky, tough-looking guy, and even with his helmet and goggles on I could see he had bushy, black eyebrows and was angry. He was hunkered down in the cockpit and obviously was going to teach me a lesson. He wasn't going to let me turn right any place in North Florida. This unfriendly, pushy attitude aroused in me a certain amount of competitiveness, or don't-dare-me-to-do-something attitude.

I looked away, just as if he weren't even there, cut the throttle most of the way, turned right toward him and waited for the crash of the midair collision. It didn't come. I never looked back but somehow or other he managed to get out of my way. He must have been pretty damn quick and it must have been an exciting maneuver. I wished I could have watched it.

If he was angry before, he must have been livid after. There were some repercussions, but since he'd taken the do-it-yourself route to discipline me, instead of the through-the-channels route, nothing too detrimental happened as a result.

By late spring 1943, I'd completed the basic courses, was designated Naval aviator and received my Navy Wings of Gold. I was never more proud of anything that had happened in my life up to then. I was then sent to Cecil Field in Jacksonville, Florida, for operational training for fleet duty in dive-bombers.

The author, in his cold-weather flight jacket at NAS Pensacola, 1943. USN

Chapter 5

Transition

Lt. Stephen Alexander, the chief flight instructor at Cecil Field, the Navy's Advanced Operational Training base, stepped out of the access door cut in the huge hangar door and swore. "What the hell is that guy doing? Christ, he'll kill himself." Alexander stopped in his tracks and watched as a flight of six SBD dive-bombers with wheels and flaps down circled the field so close in that he could read their numbers. Preparing to land, they were flying only a little above stalling speed. The leader and four others had broken off as the flight moved upwind above and to the right of the runway. They had made their left turns and were now coming downwind before turning to a landing. Tailend Charlie, the last plane, had gone too far upwind and now had his bomber wrapped up in a 50 or 60 degree bank trying to regain his position. He was low, slow and dirty, dragging around with his wheels and flaps down. Worse, he was making a turn downwind, the graveyard turn. The chief instructor watched as the plane stalled, flipped onto its back, nosed down, half spun and plowed into the ground, completely disintegrating as it did so.

Sirens screamed and horns blew; the tower exploded red warning flares into the sky. An ambulance and two fire engines roared out of their

The famous old SBD Dauntless dive-bomber with author John F. Forsyth and rear gunner Walter A. Brown. USN

ready spots and charged off, with engines blatting, toward the crash. Unexplainably, the plane did not burn, but that mattered not to the pilot. He died in his cockpit.

Within 15 minutes the bullhorn bellowed, "Lieutenant Alexander, report to the captain's office on the double." The captain was new to the base. Alexander knew he'd want a full explanation, right now. The captain would certainly take a dim view of smashing up airplanes and pilots, and just as Alexander had to report to the captain, the captain had to account to his superior, the admiral of the Training Command.

"Lieutenant Alexander, what happened? Why did it happen? And what are you doing about it?"

That's the Navy way.

"Sir, it's a matter of transition to heavy aircraft."

"Keep going."

"That young officer, Ensign Dorsey Blair, was a better pilot than most. Most fly mechanically; they pull back the stick three inches and the nose comes up some number of degrees, that's all they know. After a few hundred hours, though, they fly by feel. They become almost a part of the airplane. They don't think mechanically, they 'feel' that when they move the stick back three inches they get X degrees of nose-up. They're part of the plane. If they want the nose up X degrees then almost without even being aware of the stick they put back pressure on the stick until they get the degrees."

The chief instructor continued: "This lad was doing a lot of wrong things but he was doing one thing right and that one thing triggered the crash that killed him.

"The right thing was that he was beginning to handle the stick by feel. He knew a tightened turn required back pressure. He was bringing the stick back, feeling for that back pressure that would tell him he had enough up elevator to stay in the turn without slipping out of it, but he never felt the amount of back pressure his fingers told him he needed. He kept coming back on the stick, increasing the tightness of the turn, raising the g-forces, thus increasing the stalling speed and finally spinning in from a violent stall. That's what happened, sir."

"Why?"

"Transition to combat aircraft, sir."

"Keep going."

"These officers have just earned their wings. They have been flying the best trainer we have, the North American Texan, the SNJ. It's the perfect trainer, low wing, all-metal, 450 horsepower radial engine, and like in a fighter, the pilot sits alone. Like in a dive-bomber the greenhouse extends aft over a rear seat cockpit. It has a thirty-caliber machine gun for gunnery practice and instruments, radio and survival gear like its big brothers, but it lacks the sinew, muscle, weight, horsepower and above all the sensitivity of an operational aircraft."

"What's the difference in flying them?"

"Two things get us in trouble. The first is just plain more weight on proportionately smaller wings. If a warbird gets slow in the air and it starts to settle toward the ground you can bend on full throttle and pray, but if you don't have a hundred feet of altitude to spare you are going to wipe out something on the ground.

"The second element is sensitivity of control. The SNJ trainer has great control for training. Its controls move easily, but in every direction you move them you'll feel the back pressure. You'll know you are moving that stick and at the same time you will be aware the plane is changing attitude. It's cause and effect, felt and seen.

"Warbirds, as their speed and power increase, become increasingly sensitive. When you pour on the coal with a fourteen-cylinder engine you get pushed back in your seat. A flick of aileron and a touch of rudder rolls you inverted in a second. Pull the stick back as you might in a trainer and you'll stall and spin or black out. You have to get used to all this.

"This officer was trying, he was learning fast. He pulled the stick back, he was looking for the back pressure the SNJ would have given him. Instead he was pulling back on the stick of a dive-bomber. A plane with smooth effortless control designed to bring that plane out of a vertical dive instantly if necessary. In fact the elevator is so large and so easy to deflect that you can whip the stick straight back in straight and level high-speed flight and do a high-speed stall snap roll, in which maneuver you change the plane's direction so hard and fast that the wings stall and the plane snaps into a horizontal spin so violent and fast as to momentarily disorient you.

"Ensign Blair's plane was low, slow and dirty. He was in a fifty-degree or more bank. He came back on the stick feeling for the trainer's back pressure but the dive-bomber's elevators worked like velvet. There was too little back pressure, too little 'feel' for him to recognize it, and just as day follows night, as he tightened the turn, the bomber snap rolled and went in."

"What are you doing about it, Lieutenant?"

"Sir, our instructors are the best. They are up-to-date. We have manuals—"

"Do you have one here?"

"Yes, I brought—"

"Leave it here. I'm going to read it thoroughly. Then we'll talk further.

"In the meantime, get a recommendation from the instructor of the flight that Ensign Blair was in as to which officer to send home with the casket. It was a bad crash. The casket will be sealed and that officer will be under my orders that no-one, under any circumstances, will open that casket. That poor family has had enough trauma already.

"One thing more, Lieutenant. You now need a replacement in that flight. A list of new men reporting here for training came in this morning. One was an ensign named Forsyth who had four or five hundred hours as an instructor before he joined the Navy. He would be a logical replacement for that flight."

"Yes, sir, but if he's an instructor we need him badly right here."

"I'd like to get him for you but he came into the Navy as an officer and as such can pretty well choose his billet. He wants to go to the fleet. He has orders for dive-bombing training, so unless you can talk him out of it he goes to the fleet, as his orders say. I'll keep trying to get you more instructors."

Chapter 6

The Old Navy

The mean age of the "Old Navy" was probably thirty. They were the men who'd joined before Pearl Harbor. They included reservists, like Ben Preston and Leif Larson, and regulars—US Navy, graduates from Annapolis—like Charlie Gold, Harlan R. Dickson, Mark Eslick, Jr., and George Ghesquiere, who were captains of our squadron from time to time. All these men shared the same ideals about their country and the justice of its causes and all were ready to be the first to face the troops and air forces of an enemy.

We had the opportunity to know well the four Annapolis men and we liked and respected every one of them. However, they certainly were different from each other. Our first skipper worked from 7:45 a.m. to 4:45 p.m. and always, with great precision, made the Officer's Club Bar by 5:00 p.m.

Capt. Benjamin G. Preston, winner of three Navy Crosses, four Distinguished Flying Crosses, two Air Medals. He was a Naval aviator and leader of truly heroic proportions. B. G. Preston

Ens. Art Chauvel, an excellent officer, lady-killer, raconteur, smooth pilot and deadly dive-bomber. USN via Art Chauvel

When Harlan R. "Rocky" Dickson came aboard we never stopped working. We flew and studied all day and might be routed out at any hour of the night to go on a practice emergency exercise. This was real practice for what was to come. Rocky's approach was hard-boiled efficiency, all seriousness and all business. Where we had been used to two, three or four flights a day, depending on all sorts of conditions, we went on a new schedule of four flights a day, depending on nothing! Weather, maintenance and hangovers be damned, you did your flying and you were judged on it.

Rocky Dickson had a fertile mind. He practiced thinking like the enemy and was forever devising new procedures to fly or creating practice emergencies for us to overcome. If the weather was bad you flew instruments. If you had an extra hour you went to the pistol range or practiced instruments or navigation in a flight simulator called a Link Trainer.

Under Rocky Dickson's orders no-one practiced in a Link without being given maximum trouble by the operator. The Link would be set to simulate exceedingly rough air and it would bounce you around so you could hardly write on your chart board. In addition, the instructors would simulate flying in near hurricane winds so that navigation would be, if possible, more difficult than anything you would encounter in real life. Rocky Dickson just wanted to preserve our lives. After all, it is a chore to have to keep training replacement pilots, so make the ones you have survive.

Rocky Dickson was a short man. Even though he was just over thirty years old, his face had a salty, weather-used look. He personified personal control. He didn't raise his voice but his voice had a precise hardness and you understood every word. His own intensity and purposefulness transmitted itself to all of us and we all became much more serious.

I was one of the ensigns who was promoted to lieutenant junior grade in the summer of 1943. I felt as though I had been elevated by the pope, and even better, the skipper designated me to be one of his wingmen. I admired his intensity and was ready to do my very best to gain and keep his confidence.

The captain felt the squadron was green, inexperienced and not responding rapidly enough to the need for superior flying, so necessary to our future. He knew what to do. He called Adm. Murray Arnold, who was then in charge of the assignment of flying officers to squadrons. Rocky had been on the *Yorktown* and had fought at the Coral Sea, at Midway and throughout the South Pacific as a pilot attached to Bombing Squadron 5. The skipper of that squadron had been Arnold, then a lieutenant commander.

When Rocky called him for help, Arnold was glad to cooperate: "Rocky, I'll get you the two best pilots in the fleet today. I'll call you back this afternoon."

Arnold checked his lists, but he knew whom he would choose. Number 1 would be Lt. Ben Preston and number 2 would be Lt. Leif Larson. Preston and Larson had served under him on the *Yorktown* and he knew their abilities well. The two had been roommates there and now were flying together in Texas, shaping up a composite squadron for escort carrier duty.

Both Preston and Larson were graduate mining engineers. They were superb pilots who knew the risks but made combat flying their way of life by choice. In addition to this, they knew Dickson, they flew like him, and they shared his intensity for maximum training and maximum performance.

Ben Preston was senior enough to rate an executive officer position in a fast-carrier squadron and would have liked to have been that. In VB–18, he would be junior to three officers. Arnold said, "I know that you'd like an executive officer billet, but in VB–18, you'll be working with Rocky Dickson, helping him to make a first-class fighting machine of a raw squadron. You'll be working as Dickson's right-hand man and you'll have Larson working with you. You're the best team I can put together and you'll get back on a big ship soon, since this squadron is already into its training period."

Preston hesitated, agreed: "All right, Admiral, I'll do it."

Larson had none of Preston's reluctance and was all-out for the duty. They were on their way to VB–18 in two days. Dickson was delighted. We were impressed when the two full lieutenants, covered with ribbons and battle stars, walked into our offices and were greeted by the captain as long-lost brothers. We could sense that things were now going to get tougher quickly and they did.

Preston had joined the Naval Air Force in 1939 and Larson a short time later. Preston was thirty years old when he and Larson were ordered to VB–18. An old man we thought. He was a little above average height and sturdy in build. His hair was thinning, giving him a high forehead that glistened with dampness in the heat of the tropics. He spoke decisively and occasionally sharply if he felt the situation required. There was no sarcasm, no hidden inferences. When he spoke, you knew his mind and also, clearly, the nature of your infraction or shortcoming.

Preston had the credentials, in addition to his decorations, as he had been the aerial Gunnery Champion of the entire Navy when with the Training Command. Even more he was a great leader. We had total confidence that he'd take us into the target the best way and make it possible for us to get out after the bomb release. We could, and we did, stake our life on his cool control and judgment in emergencies.

Larson was a tall, athletic-looking Swede from Deadwood, South Dakota. He had curly, light brown hair and a firm jaw. He'd learned a lot about the war, having had to fight in the big battles. When the *Yorktown* was sunk in the Coral Sea, he had to swim off it. He always felt this was an ignominious way to leave a ship, especially when his mates, Dickson and Preston, were airborne and landed on the *Enterprise*. They not only landed on the *Enterprise*, they volunteered and joined the dive-bombing squadron there and stayed in the war until that tour of duty was over. After that, they were sent back to the States to form new squadrons.

Early in the war, after a Jap ship had been sunk, Larson came upon a lifeboat full of its survivors. He could have strafed it, destroyed it and killed the fifty or so men who were in it. But at the outset of the war, we didn't do things like that.

Later, after he'd seen his mates machine-gunned in their parachutes and lifeboats and other acts of barbarism, he'd wished to high heaven that he'd strafed that lifeboat, and when he'd had a little too much to drink and was a bit tired or depressed, he'd chastise himself for flying away from that boat without killing its occupants.

Preston and Larson had a feature in common: the bridges of their noses were scarred and slightly flattened or thickened. The feature could have come from boxing or just a plain fist to the nose.

Lt. Comdr. Harlan "Rocky" Dickson, the personification of valor, dedication, leadership and all the high principles that we all take pride in. He was killed in the line of duty, a tragic example of the gifted people of great potential whom we sacrifice in war. The Navy honored him, among other ways, by naming a ship the USS Dickson. USN

Actually, the main cause was the telescopic sight used by the early dive-bombers and fighters. The sight was mounted on the top of the instrument panel, from where it protruded to about 10 inches from the pilot's nose. In a dive the pilot could lean forward and use the sight to aim his plane at the target.

A problem occurred whenever such an aircraft crash-landed on water or land. The pilot would be thrown forward into the sight, and even though there was a thick rubber pad on the sight, he would often be knocked unconscious and would usually receive a broken nose or a bloody gash from the blow. The resultant disfiguration and scar were thereafter worn as a badge of honor by the pilot, if he survived. It clearly designated the Old Navy from the post Pearl Harbor help.

Preston, Larson and Dickson shared another principle. It was, "When you go out, use all your bombs, bullets and most of your gasoline before you come back."

One day early in the war, Preston and Larson, along with some others, strapped on their airplanes and were hurled off the deck into the air to make routine searches for enemy ships. They flew in pairs, with Preston and Larson together, on one important segment of the search.

41

That day the clouds were low, broken, gray scud. There was a higher lead-gray overcast and no sun. A drizzly, miserable day. Neither pilot had any reason to expect to see anything but a first-class combat pilot always expects to see something. It doesn't bother him in the least that "something" has not yet appeared. He expects it will appear and perhaps soon. It's the psychology of a good hunter or fisher.

Preston and Larson flew out to the farthest point of the search, not seeing anything, but still expecting to see something, and then they did see something. The surface of the dull gray-green water, sprinkled with white-caps, changed dramatically. Cutting across Preston's mist-enclosed circle of vision appeared a wide avenue of bubbly, frothy, swirling, white water. He did a double take. What? A ship's wake, of course. The butterflies flew in his stomach. It was the only time that he later admitted to prayer. He prayed, "Please, God, make it a Jap ship, a big one."

Larson had seen the wake too and his plane was fairly bouncing in anticipation. Preston rolled to the left to follow the wake. As he did so, he armed his bomb and charged his guns once more. Larson stayed glued to him.

They followed the wake and within 2 minutes they flew right up the fantail of a big ship, a Japanese heavy cruiser. Their approach had been anticipated by radar and their reception was definitely hostile.

Preston pulled back into the scud with Larson following and tried to figure out how to catch the fish they'd found. The ceiling was 600 feet, too low for a dive-bomb attack. *Well,* thought Preston, *we still have plenty of gasoline. These clouds must have some holes. We'll dog this cruiser until we find us a hole in the clouds and then we'll sink him.*

So Preston and Larson throttled back, to conserve gasoline, until they were just barely hanging in the air. Then they circled on the edge of the cruiser's visibility and waited. A half hour went by with no breaks in the clouds, but to be sure Preston would not abandon the chase, Larson signaled regularly to him that he thought the clouds were getting thinner and

Lt. Ben G. Preston and gunner Honnen stalk the Japanese fleet. USN via R. Shipman

higher. Nevertheless, to Preston, the pragmatist, the clouds were just as dark and just as rainy and just as low.

About every 10 minutes after that half hour passed both pilots would refigure how much longer they could shadow the cruiser and still make it back to their own ship. The time constraints became tighter and tighter. A little perspiration formed in a new place under Preston's helmet. He looked up from the fourth time he'd rechecked his navigation and the scud was thinning, now having some breaks and holes in it. His adrenaline kicked in. Maybe this was it and it would not be a minute too soon. He picked up the radio: "Let's get 'em, Larson."

Larson tightened up his position, bringing his wing to within 6 feet of Preston's plane. Preston poured on the throttle, pulled the nose up and climbed up through the ragged clouds to 6,000 feet, to where his back was rubbing on a solid overcast again. Not very good but high enough to make a run. He spoke: "Leif, we only have two bombs total. We need at least that to sink this baby. If you aren't right on target don't release. We'll go back up and try it again."

"Roger, Ben."

Their approach to the point of attack was greeted by every AA gun on the ship. Preston flew toward the attack point in wild gyrations and Larson stayed with him as if he had been attached with a rope. They started their dives almost together, planning to drop at 1,800 feet. Preston maneuvered his Dauntless dive-bomber into a smooth straight 60 degree dive and centered his sight on the ship's superstructure. As he approached 1,800 feet, a wisp of cloud floated across the target and Larson burst on the radio, "Hold, hold, I'm not on."

They pulled out and up in a hard-climbing turn and started back to 6,000. Preston was now facing several monsters. The first was the Jap cruiser, the second was the lousy weather and the third was the growing gasoline shortage. However, he felt they could still disable the ship.

As they climbed, they agreed that they'd use the same procedure on the second run. They'd hold if either were not on target and they'd dive together. Preston believed instinctively that two planes diving together would have more than twice the chance of surviving the dive than two planes diving separately.

They made the second dive. AA was bursting all around, tracers were streaming up from the decks, cloudlets were here and there. Preston maneuvered and then drew bead on the ship. He thought, *I've got you now, you bastard.* But at that moment, Larson yelled into his mike. "Hold, hold, I'm not on." They pulled out in a zooming roll and started back to 6,000 feet.

We have to do it now, thought Preston, and a new trickle of sweat ran down the bridge of his nose. However, to Larson, on the radio, Preston was calm and encouraging. Like a good coach, he knew not to load his man up with pressure, especially when they were both about ready to burst.

They reached 6,000 feet one more time and turned toward the ship; began their crazy, jinking dance; and took the steep ride down. At 2,000 feet Preston knew this was it. He pressed the bomb release at 1,800 feet. A beautiful dive. He had a hit, he was sure, and so did Larson. As Preston twisted through his pullout, he caught sight of two tremendous explosions on the decks of the cruiser.

With those bomb bursts, Preston felt a sense of elation—not surprise, but elation, high elation, like that which came with winning a big victory. Probably the two bombs were not enough to sink the ship but the damage had to be extreme. At the very least, the ship had to be out of action for months.

Now they had to find their ship and land aboard. They would fly to the point where the ship's navigator had predicted the ship would be at the hour they might expect to sight it. The later they were, the farther along its course the ship would be. It was like the solution of an infinitely converging triangle problem.

If their navigation was off or if, for enemy action or other reasons, the ship had not followed its projected course, the pilots would arrive at the expected rendezvous and see only an empty ocean.

In such a case, the pilots would start a square search. They would fly a distance equal to the range of visibility, then turn 90 degrees and repeat. At the end of that leg, they would turn 90 degrees again and fly twice the length of visibility, and so on, at every two turns doubling the distance of the leg. They would have a good chance of finding the ship *if* their gasoline held out.

This day, Preston could only hope the ship was where his navigation placed it. Fortunately, but more by skill than luck, the ship was there and Preston and Larson landed aboard. Each plane had used up all but a few minutes of its fuel. As the captain of the ship said, "Well done, that's the way to run a mission."

Preston and Larson seemed to us, in VB–18, to consider a man's willingness to fight any man at any time as a way to test some indefinable characteristic of their squadron mates. Obviously, they didn't want to fly with and rely on a guy without guts or without a willingness to dare risk for himself or for his leader or squadron mates.

Somehow, Preston had the impression that Walt Madden might not measure up. It was a completely erroneous impression, but Preston felt it and he said directly to Madden, "You're a coward."

Madden could not even associate such a thought with himself. When he recovered, he said, "Damn you, Preston," and the fight was on.

After a few good punches were thrown, the rest of us broke it up and sent the combatants in different directions.

However, Preston was impressed, and the next morning sought Madden out and said, "Walt, I was wrong, you're all right. I'd fly with you anytime." They shook hands and that was that.

Most of us did not become involved to that extent but I can't say Preston's approach was inappropriate. Nobody wants a reluctant pilot on his wing when his own life depends on it.

In California in the summer of 1943, after Preston and Larson joined the squadron, our lives changed even faster. With Preston and Larson to help him carry out his ideas, Dickson tightened the winch on us all another full turn.

We woke up one morning to read that henceforth, the squadron day would begin at 12:00 noon and would end at 2:00 the next morning. There would be two daylight hops and two night hops. Further, we would do every type of aerial and bombing exercise that we could do in the daytime at night, including carrier landings and dive-bombing.

From then on, we flew our two hops a day and two hops a night. We navigated out over the black ocean alone and in formations of twelve to eighteen planes. We flew instruments, we dive-bombed targets illuminated by flares that we dropped and we dive-bombed targets illuminated by flare pots on the ground.

The night flying was scary. We flew in formations so much that we were not good instrument pilots, but even if we had been, it still would have been adventurous the way we did it.

One of the most difficult parts of instrument flying is to fly half by instruments and half by visual reference to points outside the aircraft, like the horizon, the clouds or the plane flying on in the formation. Flying in formation at night required this split of concentration. It also changed your perspective and references. For instance, the plane you were flying formation on changed from a three-dimensional object you could relate to, to dim red, green and white lights. After each time you glanced at your own instruments, you had to stare at those lights and reconstruct them in your mind as an airplane, and determine if you were holding steady or moving toward or away from that airplane. Depth perception was probably nil. However, the more of this type of flying we did, the better we could do it.

Simulated night carrier landings were worse. One field had an area the size of a carrier deck marked off on the runway. A division of six planes would circle individually and bounce down on the marked area, ram the throttle forward, take off, drag around the field with wheels and flaps down at about 200 feet high, and do another landing in turn.

The planes would be low, slow and flying mushily, all of this making altitude hard to control. Fortunately, the land around this field was flat and uninhabited, because quite often, someone would get too low—low enough to take out a farmer's barn before realizing his position. At least once, a plane with wheels down flew right onto the ground and bounced back into the air, with the pilot scared silly.

Dive-bombing was the worst. All you could see was the target and there were no other visible reference points to tell you how steep you were diving or especially to warn you when to pull out. At that time the Navy was losing one dive-bomber per day in the States in practice in the daytime. Many of these losses resulted from target fixation. The pilots were trying so hard to center the target that they flew straight into it, and that was in the daytime!

The diving down was bad and so was the pullout. Because of the steep dive the artificial horizon would tumble at the beginning. This meant your main flying instrument was out and you had to pull out and level off on four secondary instruments—the needle, ball, air speed indicators and altimeter. This was theoretically possible to do, but a pretty draining operation when done for real.

After the dive we had to reassemble, then sort ourselves out into the formation we had started with. I still don't know how we did that with regularity.

The other major problem was vertigo. With vertigo you can't tell up from down or level flight from a vertical turn. It occurs most frequently in formation flying at night, when you have few reference points and must turn your head frequently, looking first at the leader, then at your own instruments, then back. This turning confuses the sensors in your inner ear, where balance is maintained, and causes vertigo.

Vertigo is an absolutely terrifying feeling. You just know you're going up in a right turn, but your instruments show you going down in a left turn, and if you don't turn right you'll be killed, but every nerve and sense in your body shouts, "If you do turn right you'll be killed!" This is paralyzing. It's disorientation at a critical time.

Ens. Delbert "Speed" Goodspeed experienced it one night. We were flying in tight formation in a moonlit, but cloudy sky, and the leader, to avoid the clouds, was making gentle turns and climbs or dives, first to the left and then perhaps to the right.

All of a sudden I saw a plane in the second section, Speed's plane, flare suddenly and sharply to the left and disappear into the blackness in a diving turn.

I shivered inwardly, Speed had a monster in his cockpit, vertigo! He had spun out of the formation, but now free of the formation, he could at least concentrate on his instruments. Could he overcome the paralysis of fear and the terror of disorientation, all without his gyro horizon; regain control; and pull back into his position?

A minute or so went by and I looked around to see if I could spot his running lights coming back in. As I looked back I saw a flash of light from down below. It was an explosion on the ground, 12,000 feet below us.

For a second I didn't comprehend. You never do. It always takes a moment when you don't want to accept what you're seeing. We'd just lost another squadron mate and friend. Speed never regained control. The monster ate him up, and together they blew a 12 foot hole in a farmer's field.

However, for all the hazards, we had fewer casualties than previously and we grew sharper, more competent, more confident and proud of our achievements. We accepted Rocky Dickson's philosophy of "Practice it the hard way, the tough way, because no matter how tough it is, the real thing will be tougher."

The best tribute to Rocky Dickson and his training, and Ben Preston's leadership, came on September 21, 1944. We were in Task Force 38.2, which included the large fleet carriers *Intrepid* and *Hancock* and the medium carrier *Cabot*.

The task force was steaming 110 miles off the east coast of Luzon, with orders to deny the use of Clark Field on Luzon to the Japs, by bombing the runways and facilities and destroying all Jap aircraft in the area. The last strike of the day had been launched late in the afternoon. This strike had been scheduled with just enough time for us to return by sunset. Ben Preston was the leader of our ship's flight of eighteen dive-bombers, six torpedo bombers armed with bombs and a strong fighter escort. We would join squadrons from the *Hancock* and *Cabot* on the attack.

Some of the bomb fuses were delayed action, designed to dig deep into runways before exploding. Others were set on instantaneous to do maximum damage to hangars, shops, parked aircraft and equipment.

Clark Field was of immense importance to the Japanese. To severely damage it would be to cripple their air operation; therefore, it was defended by Japan's best remaining artillerymen and fighter squadrons.

Preston and his pilots and the pilots from the other ships did their jobs beautifully and the field lay holed and smoking after their attack. Just as the bombers were joining up again, they were attacked by a dozen Jap fighters. Preston could see the fighters coming in from low and from high. The Hellcat escort split to meet them and a melee ensued.

As far as Preston could see, all the Jap fighters were busily engaged by the Hellcat escort, and this seemed to be the appropriate time to slip out underneath it all, and go for home. He sent his course for the carriers but had no sooner left the environs of the field when a whole new group of Jap fighters appeared to engage the bombers.

Preston weighed his alternatives. The standard procedure would be to press on toward home, defending yourself as well as you could, but if the Japs were any good you would certainly lose a few planes.

Preston chose to turn his whole formation around, going back into and under the melee. The Hellcats were very busy and I'm sure they didn't welcome Preston's return with a whole new group of Jap fighters for them to take on. But on the other hand, they were so good at keeping the Japs busy that none of the enemy had the time or inclination to try to shoot down a bomber and become fair game for the Hellcats in the process.

Every time Preston tried to leave the fight, more Japs appeared, so he stayed until the end. Finally, the fighting became scattered and a few Hellcats gathered around the bombers, to escort them, and they all started back toward the fleet. A number of Japanese fighters came along. They appeared to be escorting the escorts. They had been burned by the Hellcats and chose not to close but to tag along at a safe distance, obviously hoping for a straggler or some other break.

The fight had taken quite a bit of time. Preston took a quick look at his course and time to the ship and then a look at the rapidly setting sun gave him a jolt of concern. They'd be lucky to reach the ships in daylight.

In addition, the stay for the fight had used up a lot of fuel. It was a tough decision for the leader: speed up and burn more gas to get in by daylight, or conserve fuel to be sure they could at least reach the ships and take their chances on night carrier landings.

Preston chose to get his planes in before dark and added 30 or 40 knots to normal cruise speed to return in daylight. This was a good decision but fate held the high cards and called for an ultimate test of skill and training. The ordinary late afternoon rainstorms had combined with a nasty weather front. This front was overtaking the fleet, forcing it south and east.

Task Force 38.2, all by itself, had eight squadrons in the air and all would be low on gas. It was too much to even contemplate that we could successfully land even most of those planes, at night, in rain, clouds and fog. Preston's decision to risk getting there in daylight was the right one.

As our planes approached our ships, the ship's radars picked up a large number of bogeys (enemy planes) following our planes toward the fleet. The last thing we needed was enemy fighters in our landing patterns and enemy bombers after our carriers when they were trying to recover planes.

Our admiral, Gerald Bogan, the commander of the task force and carriers, turned his ships and headed for safety. They steamed into the bad weather and disappeared. If he had to choose between losing his ship and losing all his aircraft and airmen, he chose to lose the planes and airmen. Even we would admit that was the right decision; we knew we were expendable.

Preston's judgment in navigation and flying was perfect. He'd stayed at the target with the fighters, rather than run home and get shot down. His extra speed brought him back just before dark and his navigation hit the carriers right in the nose. But as he drew close to the ships, even having them in sight, the ships disappeared into the rain clouds to prevent the Japs from attacking them.

Preston and the planes with him took up circling again. It looked bad—so bad, in fact, that the leader of the six torpedo bombers decided the best chance they had was to stay together, not go into the bad weather and not try to land after dark on a blacked-out ship. His solution? He flew his group up to the edge of the storm, then one by one, each executed a perfect landing pattern over the open ocean. They landed near each other in the water, just as if the ship had been there. One of our dive-bombers, with Bob Clancy as pilot, had joined up on the torpedos during the dogfight and he too landed in the water with the torpedo planes.

As the seven planes sank, the crews all broke out their life rafts and floated together until along toward midnight, when they were picked up by a destroyer. By 10:00 the next morning, that one destroyer put twenty men back aboard the carrier and they were ready to fly again that afternoon. The decision of the torpedo leader was, in effect, if the admiral could write off the planes and men, certainly he could expend the planes to save the men. On balance, it was a reasonable decision, well executed.

Under Preston's leadership and with the benefit of Rocky Dickson's night flying training, however, all our planes and men made it back aboard, but it was a three-ring circus and never could have been done without Dickson's extra training.

Apparently the Japs couldn't find the ships any more than we could and they left for home. At that point, Admiral Bogan ordered the carriers to turn on their biggest searchlights and point them straight up to give the pilots a chance to find the ships and to give them points of reference to reduce vertigo and help them make their landing approaches.

I stood on the deck not believing what I was seeing. I had never seen lights on a carrier in the war zone, and I became acutely aware that there could be Japanese subs anywhere that would love to see the fleet illuminated like that.

The long fingers of the searchlights lit up the clouds and the rain and the chickens came home.

Finding the ships and landing on them were two different things. Our squadron, under Rocky Dickson's all-out training, had flown as much at night as some of the night fighters. It came aboard in regular style. All our bombers landed aboard without incident. The air was still full of planes, however, and we began taking in aircraft from the other ships. Both the *Hancock* and the *Cabot* had experienced deck crashes that delayed landings.

As time went on, gasoline became critical and pilots would break from their usual pattern and try to go aboard out of order. This would further delay matters and create consternation and confusion. We finally, after all our planes were aboard, had a deck crash. A *Hancock* plane tried to come in, missed our deck completely and ended up on our radio masts.

The radio masts were four sturdy, fabricated steel towers, located along the rear starboard side of the ship. These were rotated from vertical to horizontal when planes were landing. They projected off the side, level with the deck, and they caught and held the *Hancock* dive-bomber upside-down. The bomber caught fire. As the fire burned hotter and closer, the pilot, Lt. John Edmonds, and gunner, Joe Riley, released their safety belts. Riley was able to crawl to safety along the radio mast. Edmonds dropped 70 feet into the ocean. He had a little, one-battery rescue light but that was enough and he was picked up by a following destroyer. The fire was put out and we continued landing planes from other ships.

Eventually the deck became so full that airplanes were pushed off the bow into the ocean so that more could land on the stern.

After the last plane came aboard, we all went down to the ready room for coffee, hot chocolate and congratulations. Everyone was pleased and excited about the squadron's performance. This was an ultimate tribute to Preston's leadership and Rocky Dickson's intensity in the training program. Rocky would have loved to have seen his men perform so well, but he couldn't; he'd been killed in our training program six months before.

Chapter 7

Push back your frontiers

I was jammed down from centrifugal force into the cockpit of my Navy dive-bomber in a hard, high-g, diving left turn. I was concentrating on following the big, round tail of Walt Madden's SB2C, 50 feet ahead of me. It was turning, twisting and gyrating as he led the two of us on a wild tail chase across the sky, 10,000 feet over the blue Pacific.

Madden rolled out of the diving left turn into a wing-stressing, rolling, turning pullout to the right. As his nose came up to the horizon, he kept his stick hardover, fed in rudder and did two full, twisting rolls to the right without breaking the rhythm or skidding the plane. I stuck to his tail but there was plenty of slipping and skidding as I tried to track him. We were doing what every airman loves to do, tail chasing. It's exciting, it's hard work, it's great practice for combat and, beyond that, it's a vital learning experience that should be required for a "degree" in "aerology."

This was a day off, a day for rest and recreation. Madden and I were using it as a "fun flying day." As we started out to our planes, two US Marine Infantry corporals met us near the flight line in hopes of getting a ride in a plane. We were happy to oblige—anything at all for the guys fighting the war on the ground. We found them parachutes and gave them a brief check-out on the chutes, the intercom and bailing out. We took off on our recreation hop.

As Madden finished the double roll to the right, he pushed forward on the stick, sharply. I followed quickly, but there is a snap-the-whip effect and I had to push forward even harder than he did, lifting both my corporal and me hard against our belts and harnesses. The negative gs create a sensation right in the middle of your stomach that stays in your memory—but, OK, we wanted the Marines to remember the ride.

Madden continued his pushover into a steep, almost vertical dive and then pulled straight up, as at the start of a loop. As the dive started, I added power to keep up. There's a lag in the speed change for the second airplane. Maintaining a constant separation throughout a loop requires pilot number 2 to add power as the planes go down and to reduce power as the planes go up, or have the second plane run over the first.

As I followed Madden into the vertical climb, I reduced my power setting but cautiously. I wanted that engine working hard to give me a reserve of speed to hang onto his tail no matter what crazy maneuver he might do next. But, he didn't do anything except go straight up! The distance between us started to close—normally, then alarmingly. He wasn't going to turn! He was going up until he stopped, and with my momentum, in seconds we'd both be occupying the same airspace in a plane-shattering midair collision.

What was Madden trying to do? I had my answer in spades. His rudder deflected fully to the right. I'd never seen that happen before. At cruising speed, there would be no way he'd have the strength to fully deflect the big rudder; he was actually sliding backwards through the air. He was falling down on top of me and I was climbing vertically right into him. Worse, I was running out of air speed and in seconds would have no control and could never get out of his way. It would be a collision for sure.

I kicked full left rudder, hoping I still had enough air speed to hammerhead stall to the left and clear the 5 ton mass of metal that was now falling into me. I snapped back on the stick, increasing the rapidity of the stall, helping my plane to fall off and out of the way. Something worked, and I caught a glimpse of Madden falling past me.

Then I had my own troubles. My plane fell over backwards and free-fell toward the water, like the proverbial streamlined brick. Fortunately, streamlining helps direct the attitude in which an object falls and after a few gyrations, including a partial spin, the plane streamlined to a straight-down dive.

I pulled out gingerly and anxiously looked around for Madden. He was nowhere in sight. I took a shot of near panic and rolled to look for a splash in the water. As I did I saw him. He was below me and just recovering from a pullout like mine, none the worse for his "recreation." I joined up, and we did a little sightseeing, buzzed a beach or two and went back to the base.

I said, "For Christ sake, what did you think you were doing?"

"I just wanted to see what would happen. You know I learned a lot this morning, a lot about regaining control of a falling plane. Honestly, though, I would have bailed out except for that Marine in the back seat. I figured he might not be able to get out so I stayed with the plane. Now look, here's what you do—" And we learned a lesson about flying, one we'd never seen in our manuals.

Why do these things? What's the philosophy behind extra hops and dangerous experimental maneuvers?

Just this: Aviation is fun and useful but it's also for keeps. Military training for flying is tuned to training for disasters, emergencies, unexpected troubles and troubles compounded by intentional damage inflicted by an enemy, plus the need to remain operational in spite of hurricanes, high seas and natural phenomenon, all of which may combine against you at the wrong time and in the worst way. The best pilots constantly train to meet maximum imaginable difficulties and to know everything that can be known about the performance of their equipment and themselves.

It was important for our chances for a long life that we constantly push back the frontiers of our knowledge, that we dare to experiment, that we dare to test our planes and ourselves, that we exceed the limits that someone else has set—to learn for ourselves why and why not, and how and how not. No expert will be sitting with you in the cockpit when you meet the test. You better have done it in practice before you have to do it for real.

We constantly tested ourselves, our equipment and each other. Clarence "Chet" Rolka was my wingman until he was killed. Chet was a stocky, bright guy with curly blond hair. His father had emigrated from Poland. Chet was all-American but proud of his Polish heritage. There were no Polish jokes then. Poland ranks high, in the world's long history, for brave patriots. Poles have revolted, resisted and sacrificed unbearably for the cause of freedom, under iron rulers, for generations. They've earned respect and honor from every man and woman on this earth.

Chet Rolka was ready to give his all for his country, his family and his squadron mates. He was intense about his flying, he sought perfection and good men around him.

One day he moved in on my wing so that his left wing was only a foot away from and slightly under my wing. He wanted to push me a little to see if I dared turn toward him, which obviously would cause me to bump into him. He knew I wouldn't do that. I could have ignored him but the airflow over his wing lifted mine slightly and made me use down aileron to hold my position. It was challenging that he was so close and a little annoying that I had to keep correcting. The most he'd expected from me was a cautious turn toward him or an obscene gesture. But he put the ball in my court and I could react cautiously or test him. My mood crystallized; I accepted the challenge. I wasn't sure what would happen but I brought my wing down with a thump on his wing. He jumped a foot, pulled back a little and scowled at me. I guess that's how we established our credentials with each other.

The more frontiers of experience that could be pushed back in a simulator or simulated exercises the better. The simulation should be as true to actual combat as possible, even though, every so often, simulations go out of control.

Chet, ten other dive-bombers and I were engaged in war games off Hawaii against our own Air Group 18 fighter squadron, who were making simulated firing runs on us. We were flying in four Vs of three planes each. I led the second V and was flying a step down from and to the right of the first V. The fighters would start from ahead of and above us, six on the left, six on the right. One would dive toward us from each side and the others would follow in quick succession. Some of their passes were almost head-on, at extremely high speeds and exceedingly close. They didn't have to worry about our forward-firing cannon, since this was a simulation, and they pressed their mock attacks most aggressively.

It was only a game but they were coming so close from the front that it made us nervous as cats. As they bored in on us, I edged farther and a little farther yet under the first V. I wanted to get on the radio and back them off from the chicken game but it wasn't my prerogative.

Just then, another F6F came barreling in. He was coming from a little above us to the right, and as he pulled in at us, he was in a vertical bank aiming right at Chet Rolka on my right. It was obviously a dangerous pass. Both Chet and I slid cringing to the left. The fighter concentrated on his run to the exclusion of all else. When he finally realized how fast he was closing and how directly at us he was coming, it was too late. The plane gave a convulsive jump in its vertical bank as he pushed forward on the stick to avoid Chet's plane. He didn't make it. They hit, wing root to wing root. Neither plane exploded. Each had a wing gone, we were not high, both went into the sea. The two pilots and Chet's rear gunner, Tom Collins, died on the spot.

I couldn't twist around enough to see Chet's plane go in, but I left the formation and flew to the spot, hoping against hope for something. The crash site was marked by a slick of oil and gasoline in a 40 foot wide circle. A little debris floated in the circle and the outer rim of the circle was a ring of flames from the gasoline. There was no sign of life or of anything that had been life. I circled two or three times and rejoined the flight.

The games were called off, and we returned to base. The brass had a conference, and the fighters were given a caution—not punishment and not a new rule, but a full explanation of why and how the tragedy had happened. It was made into a learning experience, but an experience that this time was not worth the cost.

A squadron executive officer once called me a "hot pilot." He was calling me a crazy. I disagree. This occurred after he had stood with the landing signal officer, watching his flock shoot simulated carrier landings on an airfield that had the outline of a carrier deck marked on it.

Six planes were in the pattern at the time. They were flying just as if they were landing on a ship. They dragged around the field 200 feet up or less, wheels and flaps down, hanging in the air on their propellers at just above power-on stalling speed but at a high-power setting and on the reverse side of the power curve, six accidents waiting to happen.

Lt. Dick Moot, the landing signal officer (a specially trained pilot) stood at the left rear corner of the simulated deck and, with hand paddles, guided the planes from the ground as each curved in toward the landing spot. As a plane reached a precise position in the air at the right speed and the correct course, the landing signal officer would bring his right paddle sharply across his upper body, signaling "Cut!" The pilot would cut his throttle and attempt to complete the landing, or "bounce," as we said.

After landing, the procedure was to retract flaps partway, pour on full throttle, lift the tail, roll down the runway to gain flying speed, take off, retract wheels, climb to 200 feet at full power, retract flaps, and only then reduce power and start a new approach pattern. There are traps throughout the procedure. The book says, have solid flying speed before retracting the wheels or you may settle back to earth and dig holes in the runway with your propeller just before you wash out the airplane.

The book goes on, don't bring up your flaps until you have 200 feet of altitude. Reason? As the flaps are retracted, the plane will settle, possibly right back to earth. Furthermore, don't "dump" the flaps near the ground; the correct procedure is to bring them up slowly so the plane can gradually adjust to the loss of lift as the flaps retract.

The consternation of the executive officer and his group was over my improvement on the standard system. We were flying F4U Corsairs, gorgeous airplanes, but as unforgiving as a jealous lover. Rumor was that fatal crashes in practice in the States were three times as numerous in the Corsairs as in the F6F Hellcats. The Corsair had the reputation that if you bounced it off the ground on the landing and jammed on full throttle to go around again, the torque of the engine would flip the plane on its back and send you to the arms of your maker forthwith.

My system violated all taboos, regulations and rumors. When I bounced that big baby on the deck on the field, I immediately, while still airborne from the bounce, put on full throttle. You could feel it start to roll over if you were rough with the throttle, but if you moved quickly but smoothly, it would take the power without flipping upside-down and stay airborne.

As soon as I threw on the coal I would hit the wheels-up lever and cock in a little nose-up so we didn't settle and dig those holes in the runway. Then in the same breath, I did the big one. I dumped the flaps, not slowly, but all at once and fast, at about 5 feet altitude. As the flaps came up, to compensate for the lost lift and to prevent settling into the ground, I increased the angle of attack by a simple method of more nose-up. I had now hung the airplane on its engine but only after I knew the engine was putting out its power and only for seconds.

With the engine going full blast, the wheels streamlining themselves and the tremendous drag of the flaps disappearing, the plane surged ahead immediately, and I only needed a moment for the speed to build to be off and flying with a comfortable margin of air speed. The big benefit was that in a few seconds more, I could reduce from full takeoff power to climb power, instead of climbing to 200 feet at full power, as the book required. Full power chews up engines. I felt my system was a good engine-saving procedure. Was it dangerous to do or learn to do? Well, just don't try it near the ground at first. Go up to 5,000 or 10,000 feet, find a nice flat cloud layer and pretend it's the ground. Slow your hot airplane down and practice dumping your flaps or anything else right on that cloud.

The first time I tried the procedure near the ground, I already knew I could do it, and that's not being "a crazy."

In the same vein, I've flown inverted near the ground, but before I ever did that, I practiced on a flat cloud layer. I'd fly so close to it that I could dip a wing on either side and touch the cloud, then I'd pull up a few feet and roll it. I might do five or ten rolls in a row, watching my lower wing tip on every roll. I imagined that if a wing tip touched the cloud I was dead. It was only when I could do this with perfection that I tried it near the ground. So, I deny being a crazy; I knew what I was doing. I also cheated a little—for Mom. When I started a roll off the ground I cocked the nose up just a trifle so the momentum was going up and not down. Mom was pretty important to me.

I did other things, sometimes, with no good purpose except that I would learn from doing them and that if they amazed, amused or shook up my friends at the air base, that was exciting too.

My rear gunner was a diminutive young man of nineteen who answered to Brownie, partly because of his slight build and perky attitude and partly because his name was Walter A. Brown. Brownie's short Navy career had been speckled by adversity. He was too good with the cards and the girls and too unconcerned with Navy regs. I admired his independence and his fight for status among his peers and we became a team.

In some ways it was not a smart choice. For instance, because of the disparity of our sizes, how would Brownie ever have been able to pull me out of a sinking plane if I were unconscious? However, he worked hard and was good at what he did.

Brown talked a lot among the aircrews and bragged to them of the wild and wonderful maneuvers we did. When he would exhaust his repertoire of stories, he would subtly push me for another "incident" or a new maneuver. Partly as a result of this came a real showstopper. It was essentially a Split S to a Landing.

In a Split S, the aircraft follows the line of the top half of an imaginary vertical letter S. You roll your airplane upside-down and pull back on the stick, go through straight down, and pull out straight and level, heading 180 degrees from your original course. The problem is the tremendous build-up of speed, which dramatically increases your turning radius as you proceed through the vertical part of the dive. A plane like a Corsair, clean, will require more than 5,000 feet of altitude to make the turn and you never

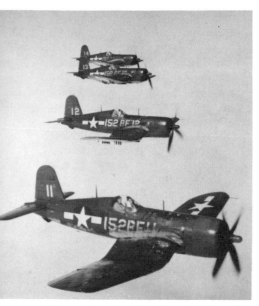

The author in his Corsair (number 11). USN

Brownie and I practiced hard. While practicing combat maneuvers over Hawaii we shredded the fabric on our Helldiver's rudder. USN

know quite how much it will use until it's too late to recalculate the amount you need. Once you get near the vertical you are committed to pull out no faster than the aircraft's maximum rate of pullout. If you miscalculated the radius needed, you're dead. It's an ironclad rule for all pilots: Don't do a Split S near the ground.

Everyone was respectful of Split Ss, or downright afraid of them. I took my day off to explore them in depth. I signed out in an SBD, found a good old cloud deck at 10,000 feet and considered that my imaginary ground level. I started the first Split S 1,500 feet above and finished 500 feet under the "ground."

I tried it again, this time with wheels and full flaps. The SBD had particularly high drag flaps—they were the lower half of the dive brakes. These were perforated more than Swiss cheese and really slowed the plane down. With wheels and perforated flaps fully extended, I lost no more than 800 feet in the next Split S. Better yet, I found my speed was, within limits, controllable; there was none of the runaway, heart-stopping, accelerating slash through the air that a Corsair, clean, makes as a dive steepens.

I played with speed and radius (pull out) control. The slower you fly the sharper you can turn and pull out. I found that air speed was more controllable at 75 degrees down than at 90 degrees down, so I leaned the imaginary S sideways 15 degrees, and now 75 degrees down from level flight became the maximum angle of dive in two of the three geometric planes of my path through the maneuver. Thus, in addition to more control over speed and pullout, I had also created an escape route 15 degrees better than 90 degrees. I still rolled the aircraft on its back to start with, then pulled the nose earthward. When seen from overhead, it was 15 degrees off straight down, but when seen from a side view, it was straight down. If at any time an emergency or miscalculation appeared, I could roll my aircraft around its longitudinal axis to the 75 degree plane and pull out in 75 degrees instead of 90 degrees. I was 15 degrees closer to escape.

One day, I watched a friend in a Corsair Split S from 4,000 feet. Of course, he didn't make it. He turned as tight as he could but he hit the ground at 400 miles per hour in a 15 degree nose-down, smearing, fiery smash. Fifteen degrees would have saved him.

Using the new technique, I could do a Split S in 800 feet of altitude, as long as I had a few thousand feet for margin of error. I could also round out of the dive near the end of the runway at 125 knots—fast but comfortable and controllable.

When I had learned all this and practiced at altitude, I was ready to try it as an approach to a landing, but it still was tense to do it for real. I knew I could do it in 800 feet, but I added another 200 feet as a margin—for Mom.

I flew downwind at 1,000 feet, over the very edge of the runway, close enough so I could barely see it under the fuselage without dipping a wing. I traveled 100 yards past the end of the runway and rolled upside-down. I looked up at the runway and thought, *It's awfully damn close.* I pushed the thought aside and paid attention to my flying. Flat on my back, I cut the throttle, popped the flaps, extended the wheels, pulled the nose down toward earth, and concentrated on air speed, altitude and the end of the runway. After every look at the air speed and altitude indicators, I mentally went through my escape procedure. If I had a problem, forget trying to land, just roll 90 degrees to the right, pull out and go around again. The rollout would point me right in front of the administration building but I was sure the admiral would rather have his offices zoomed than have his runway dug up with my airplane, and I kept going. Once the nose reached 75 degrees down and began to come up I knew I had it made and started to breathe again. I began to feel the combination of elation, relief and satisfaction that follows successful completion of any good adventure or win.

From the ground, my maneuver didn't have the flaring beauty of a division of fighters diving across the runway and pulling up in a quick succession of climbing wingovers to circle the field and land, but nevertheless almost every airman on the field stopped to watch my new landing procedure.

I did this a number of times, but unfortunately one day, my squadron commander stopped to watch. I was called in and received an outstanding lecture. Thus ended my aeronautical experiments in that area.

Cap the toothpaste tube, and if the pressure is still there, the paste will pop out some other place. If the skipper didn't want me demonstrating aerobatics over the field, I'd go someplace else. For example, while I was stationed in Groton, Connecticut, flying Corsairs, a hurricane came up from the South Atlantic and headed out for Martha's Vineyard and Nantucket in Massachusetts. I'd never been in a hurricane and felt I should push back the frontiers of my knowledge about them. I climbed in a Corsair and headed out to sea.

At first the weather was lousy, then it became grim. I was no great instrument pilot and I didn't want to fly high enough to get into intense up-and-down air currents, so I stayed down on the waves. The wind grew stronger and the rain came harder. I flew along about 35 feet over the waves, constantly alert to reversing course and retreating if it appeared that I might not be able to handle something. Today I think, *Wouldn't that have been a bit late to decide to turn?* But then I kept on.

It was raining so hard I couldn't see forward, so I opened my canopy and flew along looking out the side—just like Lindbergh, I thought. The waves were massive and mountainous. The wind was so strong that it was blowing the tops right off the waves and the spray and spume filled the air near the surface of the water. I was doing all right navigating out the side but I was getting wet from water blowing off the edges of my windshield. As some of the drops ran down my face I tasted salt. I was so low that I was in the blowing spume from the ocean's surface!

I proceeded along, alternately gazing in awe at the fury of the storm and wondering if I'd have trouble turning around. I was concerned that in a turn, I might lose a little altitude, catch a wing in a wave and—ugh.

Without warning the surface of the ocean changed instantly into surging, boiling, white froth, and a gigantic wave split halfway up its slope, rolled over and came crashing down in an unspeakable explosion. It was a breaker, breaking on a sandbar. I saw no land, but I could see only about 100 yards. I was so startled and undone by this incredible show of force by Mother Nature that I turned tail immediately and started back out of the storm.

I made it back. I'd learned more about flying. I'd pushed back a frontier. And when I had to fly antisub patrol off a carrier in the Pacific in a typhoon in 50 foot waves, I was glad for every bit of flying knowledge I had accumulated.

I joined VB-18, a dive-bombing squadron, in July 1943, at Alameda, California. Lt. jg John Morrelle was an officer in the squadron. I didn't get to know Morrelle very well because he wasn't with the squadron very long. However, almost everyone in San Francisco knew about him.

Morrelle and five others were practicing field carrier landings (bounce drill) around the Alameda Naval Air Station. It was hazy and foggy in the area—clear near the airport, foggier northward around the Bay Bridge. Morrelle had to be flying with his canopy open; it was required in bounce drill, and because visibility was so poor, he'd need to be flying with reference to the water. I'm not sure what kind of flying Morrelle had done before, but it is unlikely that he'd flown someplace, like in a hurricane, where the visibility was impaired to the extent it was that day at San Francisco Bay. He must have been uncomfortable flying so low and slow right down on the water in all that mist and fog. He was a good officer, though, and others were doing it so he was doing it.

To keep from crowding one another in the poor visibility, the six planes strung out farther and farther in the pattern until Morrelle's upwind leg took him right to the Bay Bridge. The bridge had been obscured in the fog and then suddenly reared out of the fog at him. I can share the shock it must have been, not unlike the feeling I had when the crashing waves and sandbar materialized before me out of the rain and mist of the hurricane.

Morrelle must have hit full throttle and then made a fatal mistake. He listened to the voice of safety ("Thou shalt not fly under bridges") and instead of flying under the bridge, he pulled up to go over it—if he could. It was too high; he couldn't. The plane ran out of air speed and flew into the tough vertical cables that support the bridge deck. They sheared the wings off the bomber and it fell like a stone into the bay, Lt. John Morrelle still in it.

A search was made but the currents are strong and the mud is deep and the plane was never found. Morrelle was a good pilot and a safe pilot. If he had had the time to build experience, to push back the frontiers of his knowledge by flying under the bridge as often as we all eventually did, he might be here today.

Dare to do, dare to try, dare to push back the frontiers of your aeronautical skills. When you get to the fleet, you're playing for keeps. You'll be graded simply: either you've learned your lessons well and you survive or you're dead.

A Vertical Reverse is perverse. I sit in my Waco biplane, straining to hold the aircraft in a tight, steeply banked left turn. As the turn tightens the g-forces increase; this makes the plane seem heavier to its wings. At two g's, I've effectively doubled the weight the wings must support and the stalling speed has increased dramatically.

I steepen the bank and, to hold altitude, tighten the turn again. The plane starts to buffet. I know it's on the verge of a stall and yet my air speed is fifty percent more than my power-off straight and level stalling speed. I snap back the stick and push right rudder hard, all the way if I can. The biplane shudders and shakes like an animal, and with a racking tremor stalls sharply. But instead of spinning to the left into my turn as it ordinarily would, the whole plane goes from the tight left turn up and over and down to a tight right turn. I catch it with left rudder and forward stick but too little, too late and I go spinning out the bottom of the right turn. Ruefully, I climb back up and try again and again and again. Eventually, I can go from a tight left turn, over the top, to a tight right turn, by means of a one-half snap roll—voilà, a Vertical Reverse!

It's not my best maneuver. I don't like all the uncomfortable out-of-control feelings in the plane as it goes through the performance. But the flight examiner signs off my log with a sigh and I've passed that hurtle.

Months later in sunny California, a group of VB–18 pilots were debating just how quickly one could pull out of a dive and what would happen if you pulled out even faster. We all knew about blackouts and I for one had tried redouts. But what would ultimately happen to the plane in an ultimate pullout? Would it come apart in the air?

I thought about it for two days and then went down to the flight line, picked out an SBD dive-bomber and took off to push back the frontiers of my knowledge.

I remembered the Vertical Reverses where you snap stall already overloaded wings and try to make the plane flop up and over instead of down and out as it wants to do. In the perverse reverse, you control a stall to go from one unusual attitude to another unusual attitude by means of forcing the stall and, most important, recovering from it.

For starters, I tried a couple Vertical Reverses in the SBD. A low-wing fighter or dive-bomber has none of the stability that a high-wing trainer has in stall maneuvers. I stalled the SBD hard in a 70 degree left bank, kicked right rudder as I should have and went over the top, but I couldn't check the plane and went out the bottom spinning like a dervish before I could even find the horizon. I let the spin go a turn or two more, to be sure the plane was fully into it so my recovery procedure would be effective. As I watched the earth spinning before me in a dizzy blur, I thought, *Damn, that was a quick flip from the plane.*

I tried another two Vertical Reverses, both of which turned into strange gymnastics only slightly resembling any known aerobatic maneuver. However, I gained a new respect for the instability of the low-wing aircraft and the quickness with which it spun after a full stall. I also learned that it had a saving grace: in the beginning stages of the stall, it shook and shuddered, giving clear warning that trouble was brewing. I decided to try something not quite so advanced.

It was back to snap stalls, from straight and level flight. I leveled the plane and, at cruise speed, snapped back on the stick. The nose jerked skyward, but instead of socking the rudder to it and doing a snap roll, I used the rudder to keep the plane from falling off into a spin. I punched rudder left, then right, then left. As quick as a wing would start to drop, I'd hit opposite rudder, and prevent a spin as the nose came down. It's called walking the rudder. This worked pretty well, so I increased my speed and tried it again. This worked well too.

I jacked my speed up to a high-speed cruise and snapped the stick back into my lap. The nose started up and the plane bucked, shook and danced around like a tightrope walker. I walked on the rudder, left and right to keep the wings level, and popped the stick forward. The nose dropped; the plane steadied; the air flowed smoothly over the wing again, ending the stall; and I had a smooth, steady, responsive, controllable aircraft around me once more.

I practiced some more, until I felt comfortable, felt that I could control the plane through a high-speed stall—which now seemed to be the ultimate thing that might happen in an ultimate pullout.

I was satisfied that I'd learned something that might be useful. It saved my life the next day.

Lt. Comdr. Rocky Dickson was then the skipper of our squadron. He pushed our training relentlessly. Half our flights were flown in daylight and half in darkness. We flew extra everything. Extra bombing hops, gunnery, navigation, coordinated attacks, instruments, radar, all of it. There was some grumbling but mainly because the grumblers wanted everyone else to know how hard they were working. At about this time, headquarters asked Lieutenant Commander Dickson if he would like his squadron to practice close aerial support of a Marine practice landing assault, south of us on the California coast. Dickson jumped at the chance. We were sure to learn from it, and we did.

The day to support the landings came the day after I had practiced high-speed stalls at altitude.

We flew south past Monterey along the California coast to an area where the hills rose up from the beach to 2,000 feet or more. The Marines' instructors had built a simulated blockhouse of logs on a hillside some 1,700 feet above sea level. It was our target. We would coordinate our attack with the Marines' assault. To reduce the risk to them of a wildly thrown bomb, we carried practice bombs made of sheet metal and filled with sand, no explosives. On impact, the casing would split and a puff of sand would mark the spot.

As we approached the area we saw ships just offshore and landing craft tracking up the sea with white wakes between the ships and the beach. Rocky was crisp and efficient. He located the blockhouse and communicated with the ground forces. This was a big exercise; it would be observed by top brass. It was Rocky Dickson's utmost desire to have his squadron perform to perfection, and above all, he wanted to blow that blockhouse off the face of the earth.

We came in for the run at 15,000 feet. We'd never bombed targets that were more than a few feet above sea level. We usually released our bombs at 3,000 feet, it took 1,000 feet to pull out of the dive and I needed at least 1,800 feet of clearance over the target or my own bomb (if I had one) might blast me out of the sky.

This day the target was 1,700 feet up on the hillside, and it never registered on me that my bomb release altitude should be 4,500 feet, not the usual 3,000 feet. All I knew was that the blockhouse was a very small target; it would have to have a direct hit to destroy it and I was going to get that hit for Rocky no matter what I had to do or how low I had to go. Rocky must have been of the same mind.

We started down, Rocky first, Al Ehrke second, me third and other planes after that. I rolled into my dive and looked for the blockhouse. It was a tiny target, not like a ship. I twisted and turned, trying to put it on my optical ring sight just far enough from the pipper (the bright dot in the middle of the rings) to compensate for wind and dive angle. I was close. I twisted left and back right again. Perfect. The target no longer drifted across my sight. I was right on. I glanced at the altimeter; it was passing through 3,500 feet. I should have dropped the bomb before this but I wasn't thinking about the 1,700 foot handicap we had today and stayed hell-bent for a hit in my dive.

Ehrke was smarter. Just at the time he released and with a flaring pullout slid off the top of my windscreen. Rocky was still ahead of me, going straight down. I saw him release his bomb and flare away as Ehrke had done. I looked at the target and it was close, way too close. I saw two bombs hit the ground together at the target. Impossible! How did these bombs get there so soon and together? I'd never seen this before. Something was terribly wrong. I must be right on top of the target.

The sight of those bombs striking so near and the target so close shot a bolt of panic right through me. I never even looked at the altimeter. I touched the bomb release, started to pull out and as I did so looked up through the canopy of my steeply diving airplane and saw not the blue sky but brown California hillside. I was already below the hilly terrain beside me. The terrain was between me and my future life, and close.

I yanked back on the stick with all my might. The plane responded and the nose jerked up to level. The wings shuddered and the plane shook. It was dancing on the knife-edge, its own stability gone. The pullout had been so sharp it had separated the airflow from the wings—I had done a high-speed stall like the ones I had practiced the day before.

I knew what was coming next and unless I put my nose down I would snap inverted and spin into the hill. I was only yards from the face of the hill, my nose was pointed over the top of it, yet I had to punch the nose down or die in a spin. My reflexes, honed the day before, took over. I gasped and rammed the nose down again, right at the hill. Instantly, the plane steadied and instantly I eased back on the stick and just managed to slide up and over the top of the hill, clearing it by not more than 30 feet. God, what a relief!

As I shot over the hilltop, I looked down. As it passed under the wing, all I could glimpse was a small patch of the brown grass and, strangely, it was burning fiercely. I'd seen no fire as I dove. What was this? Oh! It had to be an airplane. Someone had gone in. Erke? No, he pulled out high. The skipper, Rocky? Oh, yes! It had to be. He'd gone low like me. He had wanted that hit. He had tried to pull out of the ultimate dive. He did the high-speed stall, but without the practice I'd had, he flipped inverted, hit the hill and exploded. It was a numbing, stunning, loss. It will always be with me and will always be total justification to me for all my experimental, adventurous extra flying and dare to do.

Chapter 8

Mousetrap

Where does a combat pilot get his smarts? Some of it comes from the football field.

You're a big husky kid. You play tackle on your alma mater's red-hot football team. You're on a high; you have just dumped two of the interference and smashed the ball carrier for a loss. You feel like King Kong.

You line up again. When that ball's snapped you're going to bust in there like a tornado and tear the ball carrier apart.

"Hike."

The ball goes, you spring forward with every bit of strength you have. You smash your shoulder into the guard in front of you and charge ahead, low to the ground, head up, legs driving. The ball carrier's coming straight at you with no blockers. You are going to crunch him for a 5 yard loss. Three more steps and—WHAM! BAM! Two burly linemen driving shoulder to shoulder have hit you from the side like a steamroller and knocked you flying from the play.

It was a trap, the mousetrap, a sucker play. The guard let you through the line, the two big boys pulled out of the line to get you. They planned it that way and together they let you have it. The ball carrier went through your now-wide-open position and that was it. You pick yourself out of the mud to try again.

When I left college and football to fly carrier planes for the Navy in November 1943, the coach gave me his best advice and final warning: "Jack, when you're in combat, don't get mousetrapped, don't fall for a sucker play. You don't get a second chance out there." I wish I could have followed his advice.

A year later, far out over the Southwest Pacific, I was flying a Curtiss Helldiver in tight formation with eleven other dive-bombers. The carrier-based helldiver had a huge radial engine on the front end, a long cylindrical fuselage and a silhouette dominated by a tail fin large enough to steer a battleship. We were packed in with a group of the new Grumman Avenger torpedo bombers, while an assortment of Navy fighters crisscrossed over and around us.

This was it, my first real attack on an enemy. An enemy with real guns, an enemy who would do everything a man could do to kill me. I wasn't afraid but I was a bit scared. To be scared is to be alarmed, to be afraid is to be filled with fear. There was danger ahead, yes, but I was the hunter, the aggressor, the person in control. They had to be afraid, not me. Ah, the misconception of inexperience.

Helldivers return to the carrier after a mission. USN via R. F. Dorr

Ahead lay the target, an airstrip on the island of Peleliu in the Palaus. I'd never heard of such a place, and even today, I can't pronounce the names accurately enough to get me local guidance to its airport.

Six months before, the island had been a Japanese storage base well defended by experienced airmen and troops. At that time the islands had been heavily attacked by our carrier squadrons and reduced to a shambles. Had they resupplied their forces? Would it be a real tough go or a piece of cake? We were sent in to find out.

The airfield assigned to my squadron to bomb was a strip bulldozed through the palm trees with buildings half hidden by tall coconut palms along one side. The Japanese were there. They knew we were coming and their guns were loaded.

As we approached the target I mentally went through my diving checkoff list. I charged my 20 millimeter cannon with live rounds. They were incendiaries and explosives; no armor-piercing rounds today. I opened the bomb bay doors and toggled the switches that armed my bombs. I reached for the latch of my canopy to open it. The air-pressure-caused vacuum of the slip-stream held the canopy in place and it resisted. I gave it a yank and broke the vacuum, and it slid back with a rush. Now the 200 mile per hour slip-stream surged into the cockpit. The full roar of the engine drowned out all other sounds. Air blast and engine noise or not, I wanted that canopy open. I might have to get out in a hurry somewhere along that vertical bomb run.

I flipped on the combination gunsight and bombsight, and two concentric circles of bright orange lines appeared on my windscreen with a bright dot, the pipper, in the very center. The circles were projected on infinity; they appeared to be at or on the target rather than a device of the plane. The sight was fixed to the plane, however, and to move the pipper you moved the plane. To bomb accurately you allowed for the wind, the angle and speed of the dive, the trajectory of the bomb, the speed and course of the target, and the kitchen sink.

The weight and speed of the plane plus the briefness of the dive created a great need for skill, muscle and promptness in correcting the path of the dive.

As we approached the pushover point the leader of the first section of three planes went first. This was the skipper's job. He signaled with an "I'm leaving now" wave to his wingman and then soared up, over and straight down to take his bomb to the Japanese gunners on the ground below.

Other planes followed in quick succession. Then came my turn. I took a deep breath, gave a final tug to tighten my seatbelt and crash harnesses, pulled back on the stick, rolled in left aileron, fed in left rudder, and soared up and over in a smooth curvilinear rolling wingover. As I reached the inverted position, with the airstrip now directly over my head, I popped open the dive flaps.

The trailing edge of the wing appeared to split apart as the brakes opened, standing out like walls from the top and bottom of the wing. The plane slowed as if it had flown into thick glue. With the drag of the dive brakes, the plane could dive vertically downward at full throttle without accelerating beyond control. The slower speed and greater control gave the pilot time to do his job and a platform from which to guide his bomb. It also made him an easier target for the antiaircraft cannons on the ground.

As my dive flaps opened I pulled the nose farther down and opened the throttle wide. The plane surged ahead toward its terminal diving speed.

My plane was now pointed almost straight down but inverted, upside-down. It had to be; I needed to get into that dive quickly and the fastest way was to roll her over and pull down the nose. That gave me the quick entry, but now what? Simple. I just pushed my back against the armor plate behind me and rolled the plane 180 degrees. Now I was right-side-up, just about on target and building up speed like a banshee toward 300 miles per hour, straight down.

Back at the ship the man had said, "Go for the guns. They're at the corners of the field. Bomb them out and we'll beat up the base at our leisure."

In my dive I could see a cluster of three round fortified gun pits. I banked and rolled and put the center of my sight right on those guns. I was the hunter, I was trying for a good shot, I had forgotten all else. I released my bomb and pulled out of the dive, still the hunter, excited, aggressive, willing to win the war that day.

I reached down and rammed the bomb bay door lever to the closed position. As I raised my head, the air base buildings were there, right in front of me. They lined each side of a seashell-paved road through the palm trees.

Japanese targets right in front of my 20 millimeter cannon! I threw away caution and my brains went out the window too. I roared down to treetop level and sat on the triggers of my cannons. I started down the street with everything firing. It was intense, exciting and satisfying to see those tracers going out from my guns.

Tracers?

Christ, there were tracers everywhere! Zip-zip zip-zip! They seemed to go through my cockpit, in one side and out the other, in between me and the dashboard. No! They were crossing directly below the plane, maybe 4 feet below it. There were tracers from the right and tracers from the left. They had my speed exactly; they crossed right where I sat, but a little low. I was flying so low that to the gunners, the shells seemed to be going right into my plane, but because of the curving trajectory of the shells, they were arching downward and going just below me. There was no question now about whether I was afraid or scared—I was both. I wasn't the aggressor, I wasn't the hunter, I was the hunted.

I yanked the stick back for all I was worth, sank a rudder pedal to the floor and slammed in full aileron. It was probably the most unusual and violent maneuver those Japanese had ever seen. I'm sure I could never duplicate it.

The plane must have looked like a corkscrew. I looked out sideways to find and avoid the guns and my heart froze. My dive flaps were still wide open. Instead of racing full-out through the Japanese base I was sitting there at maybe 120 knots. God! I was not only the hunted, I was a sitting duck!

It was worse than that. I'd been mousetrapped, lured into a sucker play to be double-teamed by the opposition. I'd done it on my very first combat dive and my football coach had called it! Oh, miserable! Oh, lucky! Oh, eager, greedy, stupid! I collapsed the flaps, gyrated and junked my plane back to the nearby ocean, then joined up with my squadron, so relieved, so thankful, so chastened.

Chapter 9

Formosa, the first day

On October 12, 1944, in the skies over Formosa, I perfected a new maneuver and used it four times to the bewilderment of all who saw it. I've come to call it the 180 Degree Vertical Reverse and Combined Inverted Half Snap Roll. It's a doozy. I never could have done it if I had not been an instructor in aerobatics before joining the Navy.

I don't recommend the maneuver—first because it would take the wings off anything but a dive-bomber and second because the first time I did it I ended up flying head-on at a Japanese fighter who was in the process of coming straight at me with all guns blazing.

At this time the war was getting hot. The admirals decided that we should bomb Formosa (Taiwan). This was almost like going after the Japanese homeland. The Japanese had been on Formosa for fifty years. The island was like a piece of Japan, defended like the homeland and, like the homeland, something we knew nothing about.

We had had a briefing and would have laughed if it hadn't been for real. The only map we had showed large areas marked Unexplored. The only reconnaissance photo we had was a snapshot taken by a tourist in 1920 that had been reproduced in a grammar school geography book. Don't ever tell me we don't need a CIA.

Formosa lies only 100 miles off the China coast. It has 13,000 foot mountains, with the eastern shore rising steeply to the peaks. The western slopes are gradual and the land along the western coast is flat and green with cultivated vegetation. The island is alive with air bases—the unsinkable carriers of the Japanese interceptors.

The sky was still dark on the morning of October 12, 1944, when the bullhorn sounded the call "Pilots, man your planes" and the *Intrepid* commenced launching a fighter strike force to challenge the ready and waiting fighters of the Japanese Army and Navy Air Forces based on northern Formosa.

Every 10 seconds, one after another of our fighters pounded down the deck and lifted off into the blackness. We in the dive-bomber ready room, right below the flight deck, were having a disagreement over the tactics to use on our target. The target was Kiirun Harbor. Kiirun was the port of Taipei. Taipei was a big city, the capital of Formosa. The harbor was really a deep river flowing down from Taipei through a rather narrow valley, delineated on each side by steep ridges.

We could expect the riverbanks to be lined with ships and warehouses, and we could expect the entire length of the river to be heavily defended by AA batteries, probably located in the hills that ran the length of the river.

F6F Hellcats launch off the Intrepid.

The lieutenant who was to lead the second six-plane division was giving the briefing and was instructing us from where to make the attack. He picked a point where the river narrowed and said, "We'll start here and dive downriver."

I looked at the old map we had. I could visualize that valley, I could see the guns arranged along the sides of those hills waiting for us. I didn't want to be in that valley one moment longer than was necessary. I said, "Let's dive at right angles to the valley, get in, drop our loads and get out."

It was a pretty strong opinion to be voiced by a lieutenant junior grade. The full lieutenant reacted quickly.

"No way—we'll dive down the valley. That way you won't get all tangled up in the hills."

"Lieutenant, the hills are stationary," I said. "We can avoid those. We should dive across the valley to reduce our exposure to those guns. We should do anything but fly down that valley. We're not on a sightseeing trip."

My touch of sarcasm decided the issue—against me. The skipper, Lt. Comdr. Mark Eslick, Jr., stopped the discussion then and there, saying, "We'll do as the lieutenant has recommended," and that was that—except it wasn't that. Commander Eslick was killed 2 hours later as we flew down, not across, that valley.

The time came to launch the first bombing strike. Twelve dive-bombers, twelve torpedo planes equipped with bombs not torpedoes and twelve fighters were in the strike.

At the launch each plane was taxied up the deck, moving in its turn toward the takeoff spot, guided by hand signals from the launch crew on the deck, handed off from one another as it moved forward.

As you near the takeoff spot your mouth becomes dry and the butterflies flutter in your stomach. You jockey into the spot. The launch officer stops you with an open palm and an outstretched left arm. He gives you a thumbs-up signal with the right hand—it's really a question: "Are you ready?" You give him back the thumbs-up. He orders you to full power on your engine by whirling his right arm in circles, faster and faster. You hold

Grumman Avenger torpedo bombers. The Intrepid's *Avengers carried bombs, rather than torpedoes, during the raids on Formosa.* USN via Intrepid Museum

hard on your brakes and advance the throttle to wide open. The engine reaches its absolute maximum power in a pulsating, throbbing crescendo of sound. The officer throws his arm straight forward, pointing down the deck. You release the brakes and start to roll.

You look at the short deck space ahead of you and the doubts come riding in. Did they allow you enough room? Are you too overloaded? Is the engine really developing all its power? Is the ship running a little slow or the wind a little light so that you may not have the full help of the wind over the deck?

You push the stick forward to get the tail up to streamline the wings, reducing lift, which reduces drag. Maybe that will help you eke out another 5 knots by the time you get to the end of the deck. If you go to the end of the deck with the tail up, the wings will not be fully lifting and you'll roll off the deck, and into the water, no matter what else you do.

Therefore, as you reach the end of the deck you pull your stick back. The tail goes down, and you feel the tail wheel bump the deck. Now the wings are generating lift. You go off the deck, nose high, and become airborne—but airborne in a most unpleasant, slow, unstable, nose-high position, staggering in the air with full power, fighting to gain a few knots more for decent control of the plane.

Every pilot knows that at a time like this the last thing you do is make a turn, but turn is exactly what you have to do in this man's navy. The next plane will be taking off only 10 or 12 seconds behind you and if you fly straight ahead it'll fly into your prop and wing turbulence and probably be knocked inverted into the water. You must make a right turn the moment you clear the end of the deck or you've killed your buddy. So we do this. Every plane makes that clearing right turn even before the wheels are up. Then as the wheels retract, the plane surges ahead, the ailerons and rudder become alive and responsive, and once more you are flying a stable aircraft with sensitive controls that work—or else you're in the ocean, maybe upside-down trying to get out of your sinking aircraft and hoping if you make it that the ship won't run you down. You can just see and feel those 20 foot diameter propellers coming straight at you.

The skipper takes off, makes his clearing turn and then flies his takeoff heading, climbs to 1,000 feet and levels off with air speed steady at 150 knots. Six minutes out he reverses course and as he comes back toward the ship I complete my U-turn and join up on his port side. I pause for a moment to let our relative movement settle down and then with gentle pressure on my right rudder and stick I slide smoothly down and across, under him, and come up and stop ten feet from his wing on the starboard side.

I like where I am. The skipper told me he wanted me to fly on his wing and I am proud of being there.

The skipper, Lt. Comdr. Mark Eslick, is a good man, fair and honest. He's an Annapolis graduate. The Navy is his life. He's not a showoff. He's conscientious and he's dedicated to the cause, dedicated to his squadron, dedicated to us.

I know he has to worry about his position as the flight leader; he has to be the first to dive on every target, the first to bear the brunt of the cannons below. He has a wonderful wife at home. I hate to see him go in first, alone, each time. I do my best to go in with him. When he starts his dive I don't wait a safe interval, as we've been taught. Unlike some of the squadron, I go with him a split second later. If he's 50 or 100 feet ahead of me, even in a vertical dive, there is a fair chance that I won't run into him, and by being with him, I've doubled the targets for the gunners to aim at, I've added an element of choice that may be confusing to them. I just know our chances are better that way, and for my comfort, I know Charlie Draper, the skipper's other wingman, didn't delay either. He's right back of me somewhere, supporting and close.

We're now proceeding toward the northeastern shore of Formosa, another place the Japs believed we'd never reach. A place they now intend to defend with ferocity, determination and sacrificial fanaticism.

The sky is full of clouds, some low, gray layers and many higher, puffy gray-white clouds. To help keep us together the skipper flies us at 5,000 feet just under the flat bottoms of the lower clouds.

As we approach the area where we might expect to see Formosa, we see nothing. Ahead to the left, the air is hazy, thick and ominous looking. As we proceed I become aware that there is something strange and sinister about the darkening clouds in that direction. They grow even darker. They are not the dark blue-black of a thunderstorm, they are a dark green and a hard dark gray color. At times they almost seem to have a texture, with eerie-looking striations.

I turn, study this weirdness and suddenly realize I am looking at the most awesome piece of geology I have ever seen. It is solid dark green and dark gray rock. It rises vertically from the sea and goes upwards, without a break, to and through the clouds, which are a full mile above the ocean's waves. It stretches from horizon to horizon. I feel dwarfed, physically and mentally. I feel insignificant, tiny, minuscule, impotent. This thing makes goose bumps rise on my arms and the hair tingle on the back of my neck. It is dark, hard and menacing. In a word it is awesome.

We turn more to the right to skirt this wall and begin to climb. Eventually the wall and the mountains behind it, which we occasionally glimpse through the clouds, become lower and we pass over and around the northern part and proceed southwesterly across the northern tip of Formosa, close now to our objective, Kiirun Harbor.

As we fly on, in and around the clouds, it becomes more and more difficult for the second division of six dive-bombers to stay in tight formation with the first division. The leader of the second division, Lt. Ed Eisengrein, tries hard to stay with us. The skipper banks steeply around a billowing, towering cloud and suddenly the second division is gone. We've lost contact. The torpedoes were flying on the second division and they're gone too. So are the fighters—all gone, hidden somewhere around us in the clouds. We have six planes left to carry out an attack designed for at least six times that number.

How do we dare attack that target now?

The skipper may be upset, I'm furious! That division just had to stay with us. This is no picnic, they had no choice, they had to hang in there, like glue. It didn't matter if the leader had to maneuver so hard to stay with us that he lost every wingman he had, at least he would still be with us—and I know, if he had stayed with us the wingmen would have stayed on him.

Later I cooled down. Ed Eisengrein was no coward. By now we had all been tested. Additionally, he certainly did not want to separate from the skipper and further divide our meager forces, because at the time we were flying in and out of instrument conditions. Eisengrein had to follow the skipper visually and stay with his every move. He also had to keep referencing his own instruments or get vertigo and lose his whole division. It could have been in that second or two when Eisengrein glanced at his own instruments that the skipper entered a cloud and just disappeared. It was a bad break and in wartime that translates to men killed.

So now we six were alone going after the toughest target yet assigned to us. Would the skipper regroup somehow? Would he pick an easier target? Not Commander Eslick. He was true to the traditions of Annapolis, his training and the Navy service. We were going to hit the center of that heavily defended target right on the nose, we were going to do our maximum damage and then, if God was willing, those left would go back to the ship. We had another battle to fight the next day.

This day, all day, things became worse and worse. Because of the heavy clouds we couldn't make our screaming near vertical dive out of the sun. The cloud ceiling over the target was only 2,200 feet, we'd have to make some sort of a makeshift, dangerous shallow-angle run. Even if we could get to the target without being shot down the bombing accuracy would be terrible. We knew quite well the trajectory of a bomb dropped from a 70 degree dive or even a 45 degree dive but only God knew where that bomb would land when released from a 20 degree dive. Further, without delayed action fuses on the bombs we didn't dare go low or we'd blow ourselves, or the plane behind us, out of the sky.

How Commander Eslick ever found the assigned target under the clouds I'll never know but we reached the river and started down toward the harbor area. We were circling the area at 14,000 feet when we saw a hole in the clouds and made a dive for it. It was almost like a dive-bomb run in formation. Charlie Draper and I glued ourselves to the commander's wing tips as he led us down and around the ragged clouds and through canyons of angry-looking gray clouds, until we popped out of the cloud base at only 2,200 feet above the rugged terrain.

But we were over a river! *The* river! The objective, Kiirun Harbor was right ahead. I could look ahead and see much of the harbor. Warehouses covered the riverbanks, war material was stacked and parked everywhere. The docks were lined with ships—a whole row was doubled up, tied side by side along the docks. It was an unbelievable convergence of targets.

We were coming right down the docks. I hated to ignore the warehouses and the docks but those ships were so tempting and so important. I might get two with one 1,000 pound bomb. I lined up and came down the double row of ships. I picked the last row of two, leaving the closer ones for the other guys. I pushed over and started a very shallow dive from the 2,200 foot cloud base.

I was aware of tracers flying by like Roman candles on the Fourth of July. I concentrated on the ships. I didn't want to be short. I wasn't. I threw my bomb 200 feet ahead of the entire two lines of ships. It blew a tremendous hole in the water, which lasted a few seconds, and that was it. I couldn't believe I'd gone through all this to do that. Stupid idiot! I jinked to the left but the tracers were so thick that I slammed back to the right, which was no better.

Things got worse. I rolled left violently and caught a glimpse of the harbor water below me. There was a 50 foot wide circle on the water. It was as though someone had just dropped a 2 ton stone into the harbor with the circle of waves expanding rapidly outward. What the—oh, damn—damn, damn! The circle of waves! The plane ahead of me had just gone in! Who was ahead of me? The skipper! It couldn't be—but it was. He died in that cursed valley.

The harbor widened. Nobody was in front of me, so I was the leader. I looked back thinking to make a turn so the flight could join up on me. As I looked another dive-bomber spouting flames from his wings crashed into the harbor. They had gotten another one of us. Now only four were left.

Things got worse. At that moment coal-black, ugly, deadly looking Japanese twin-engine fighters appeared in our formation. They were diving and twisting right along with us. Good God, now this!

Ens. Gene Schumacher was flying last in our line of four and he was in trouble. Two of those murderous-looking, grim, black twin-engine fighters were on his tail. Schumacher's gunner's twin .30 caliber machine guns were no match for the massed heavy machine guns of the fighters. Somebody had to do something. That somebody was me, and that something, invented on the spot, was the 180 Degree Vertical Reverse and Combined Inverted Half Snap Roll. I was flying at high speed but I pulled straight back on the stick, hard. The nose came straight up and over. I'd done a tremendously tight 180 degree turn in the vertical plane. Now I was upside-down, going right back down the line of our planes and just over their heads.

Believe me, this would have been a poor position to shoot from, although the Germans were doing it against our Flying Fortresses over Germany. The solution was a quick rollover as my plane came down to the horizontal-but-inverted position. At that point, I sank the stick all the way forward and kicked left rudder. The plane did a violent half snap roll. I caught it with the stick and opposite rudder, and wonder of wonders, I was right-side-up, flying right down the line of dive-bombers, but of course in the directly opposite heading. I planned to zing just over Schumacher's head and shoot those two black monsters off his tail.

To this day I have no idea what I thought I'd do after that. I undoubtedly couldn't burn that first fighter or even touch the second one on a quick head-on pass and what would I do when they turned around to get me. I couldn't stay in the ring with one fighter let alone two, and of all things, I was now heading back toward their base and my buddies were going like hell in the opposite direction back out to the sea. I was about to be as alone and vulnerable as a bomber could ever be.

As I raced back one of the fighters broke down and away. Schumacher's gunner, Bob Christofferson, got credit for shooting it down. The other fighter was locked on Gene Schumacher's tail but now he had another plane—me—and my 20 millimeter cannons to contend with. The whole nose of the fighter flickered like a snake's tongue as his machine guns chattered and roared at me. I sat on my trigger and charged right at him. One helluva way to play chicken. Every nerve in my body said "turn, turn quick—turn!" but my adrenaline was sky high. He'd have to say uncle first, and he did. I would have ducked in another instant but he did it first. He broke down and away and I sailed over his tail.

I have no idea whether I hit him or not but as I shot past him the gravity—stupidity, if you wish—of my own situation hit me like a kick in the face. Without even thinking and in sheer desperation, I hauled back on the stick and did a second straight-up Vertical Reverse turnaround, rolled or snapped out and took off after my buddies. The Jap may have tried to reverse course to get me. I'll never know. My turn was so sharp and sudden he probably thought I just disappeared into space. In any event neither fighter came back after me and I'll never know why.

I bent on full throttle and did all I could to rejoin the other three. Charlie Draper was now the lead plane. He reached the rendezvous point just beyond the harbor and started a 360 degree turn to let the others join up. I looked beyond him and had the same sensation that I might have watching an enemy jab a long sharp hunting knife into my bare belly. Three single-engine Jap fighters had burst from the clouds and now roared at our four strung-out dive-bombers—a disaster in the making. The Jap leader may have been aiming at the second of our planes, I don't know, but as he flashed by, Charlie Draper turned sharply into him and pressed the trigger of his 20 millimeter. The leader exploded in a ball of flame. The two remaining Jap fighters pulled up and disappeared among the clouds. Draper completed his 360 degree. The four of us joined up and headed for home. As I drew up to the three remaining bombers I could see that the leader of the second section, John Gruenewald and his gunner, Mike Benak, were missing. They were never found.

Without Gruenewald, I was the senior officer and led the flight toward our check point, the big cliff on the north point of Formosa. And things became worse. That cliff was the rendezvous point for all the Jap fighters in north Formosa. They gathered there to intercept us on the way in and on the way out.

Air battles went on all day at that point. Our own Hellcats shot down forty-six aircraft in that one day in that vicinity. We four bombers, without fighters, were naked, exposed, vulnerable. The thing that saved us at that nest of fighters was our own errant, and lost to us, second division of bombers, along with the torpedo planes and fighters. They reached the check point just before us and all the Jap fighters at the rendezvous point left to attack them.

After separating from us, Lieutenant Eisengrein, the bomber leader, hadn't been able to find a hole in the clouds for the attack on Kiirun Harbor, and after flying around for a while, he started for home. As they approached the rendezvous, Zeros were waiting for them. The Hellcats and Zeros mixed it up and battled off to the north. Almost as soon as the fighters disappeared another whole group of fifteen to twenty Zeros and Tonys came up to the rendezvous point and pounced on the twelve Avengers and six Helldivers now without fighters. The bombers packed in together and used every gun they had to repel the Japs.

The air battles of the past four months had taken heavy toll of Japan's experienced pilots. The few that were left were being saved for defense of the homeland. Lucky for us the fighters we encountered that day must have been inexperienced. Their tactics were good but they failed to capitalize on the advantages they had, and not one of our dive-bombers or torpedo planes was shot down in that fight, although it lasted almost back to the ship.

When the four of us arrived at the cliff the main swarm of fighters was chasing our second division of bombers and our torpedo planes, for which we were thankful. But as we came by, two more Jap fighters reached the rendezvous point and came after us. We were flying at 2,500 feet. The two fighters flew off to our right side for a minute or two and, after examining the four sets of twin machine guns of our rear seat gunners, decided against an attack from the stern.

One of the fighters held his position. The other put on speed, pulled out in front of us and, from low down near the water, started a head-on run at us. He didn't seem to realize that from where he approached us he would look into eight 20 millimeter cannons.

As he came we lowered our noses and flew right at him. Another game of chicken; I couldn't believe it. He started to fire and so did we. I'm sure each of us felt that he had picked our own plane as his target and would shoot us apart.

Behind the windshield of our planes was a 2 inch thick piece of highly tempered glass, put there to deflect incoming bullets. The bullet-deflecting glass was only 10 inches wide and 15 inches long, but when we played chicken that day, I think I hid my whole upper body behind that one piece of glass.

This particular Japanese pilot, perceiving that on this attack the firepower was on our side, broke off the game and as we closed, he flared up and off to our right. We wrapped up our four planes in a hard right turn, trying to bring him down. I could see two exploding shells from my wingman, Charlie Draper, hit the fighter's rudder, but I'm sure that did no serious damage, just put a scar on the plane to tell his grandchildren about.

By the time we had shot at this fighter I was on a real adrenaline jag. I was so elated that for the second time that day I'd played the game of chicken and won, that I confused those small victories with vanquishing all Japs everywhere.

With adrenaline shooting through my system I executed another 180 Degree Vertical Reverse and Combined Inverted Half Snap Roll to chase the fighter we had just hit—completely forgetting that the fighter hadn't been damaged in any way that impaired his physical ability to shoot me down and that the second fighter, when I last looked, was sitting right beside us a few hundred yards out.

To be a little fair to myself, when all four of us had started to turn right to shoot at the Jap, I had expected that all would turn with me after him. But that wasn't a smart thing to do, and the others realized that and turned back to our original course rather than turning 180 degrees.

Besides, I'd gone so fast, with my violent maneuver, that they had hardly seen me go (they were still trying to shoot the Jap down), let alone had enough time to follow me. I suspect that the fighter who made the attack on us and was hit decided to go straight home, and as he flashed by us perhaps his buddy was already turning around to stay with him. But I didn't know that and I was shaking in my boots. I was humbled. I'd been so lucky. I'd better be good from now on because I couldn't count on this kind of luck everyday to bring me home alive.

I caught up with the others again and assumed the lead. We were now out over the ocean, winging away from that north tip of Formosa. I was trying to plot my course to where our ever-moving ship might be with one eye, and looking out for Zeros with the other.

Two more fighters appeared off our starboard wings. Damn them! Here they come again, get ready! Glory be, no, they're good guys! Two blue-black US Navy Hellcats pulled in beside us. They were the best-looking, most beautiful thing I'd seen all day. Maybe our worries were over. But not yet. The Hellcat leader pointed straight ahead, hopefully toward where the carrier might be, and then to our wondering eyes he and his wingman released their big, fat, external auxiliary fuel tanks, which dropped harmlessly down toward the sea, twirling slowly in the air as they went.

The fighter leader gave me the good-bye wave off and put on full speed, surging ahead, and in short order they disappeared in the haze in the direction of where the carrier should be. I felt like a leper, like a little boy whose mommy had just left him alone for the first time. Obviously, I now thought, our fighters had had a day of it. They'd used up most of their gas and probably all of their ammunition and were going home. They didn't break radio silence but they sure communicated to us that we were in hostile territory and we better get moving as fast as we could. We already had the message. This final touch penetrated like bullets and all of a sudden I was so nervous and jumpy I could barely use my plotting board to plot a course home.

It had been a terrible day. I'd carried my bomb through hell and the Fourth of July and then missed everything when I dropped it. In one hop we'd lost a third of the planes in our division. The skipper, Mark Eslick, had been killed and so had John Gruenewald, and in other flights, Ernie Benak, Don Cooper, Jim Cropper, Frank Haynes, Fred McCreary, Fred Navas, Elmer Nutgrass, Andy Rohleder and Ted A. Smith had all died.

The Japs then proceeded to attack the ship all night. It was estimated that during our three-day stay off Formosa, over 1,000 planes had been sent to attack the fleet. We lost twenty percent of our squadron's planes. It was estimated that over 500 airplanes were shot down or destroyed on the ground during the time of our raids against Formosa.

In the month of October 1944 alone, the three squadrons of Air Group 18 lost twenty-two pilots, nineteen airmen and fifty airplanes.

The bright spots for me were that I'd made head-on runs at two Jap fighters and they had both ducked first and Gene Schumacher was lavish in his thanks for my run that chased off his attacker.

With the skipper gone, the executive officer, Lt. Comdr. George Ghesquiere, became the new skipper of the squadron. He called me in. He told me that from now on I'd fly in his division. I'd be the leader of the second V of three dive-bombers. My own command, as it were. That was exciting.

That evening the new skipper served notice that he wanted an all-out effort by everyone on the morrow. He delved into the circumstances of Commander Eslick's death and to emphasize his determination that all pilots would exceed themselves he personally spoke to many of the officers. He went to Lieutenant Eisengrein, who had tried but had been unable to maintain contact with Commander Eslick's six planes during the approach to Kiirun Harbor, and said, "Lieutenant, your division was not scheduled to fly tomorrow. I'm changing that. At dawn tomorrow, you will fly the first strike. I will lead that strike. I will expect the very best from your division."

At daybreak, on our second day over Formosa, Lieutenant Commander Ghesquiere led that first strike. I led the three planes of the second section. Lieutenant Eisengrein led the second division of six planes. Everyone did his best. All planes returned but one; that one was Lieutenant Eisengrein's. He and his gunner, Jim Cropper, died together that day on the far side of Formosa.

VB–18's Ben Emge, Ernie Smith, John Gruenewald and George Ghesquiere. Smith and Gruenewald were killed at Formosa.

Chapter 10

Formosa, the second day

Every pilot and gunner had their own little private talk about how and when to get out of a burning, disabled, uncontrollable, heading-for-a-crash Helldiver. The pilot made an unwritten pledge that if there was any possible way he could warn the gunner that he was about to jump from the aircraft, he would do so, even if it meant delaying his own jump, or increasing his own risk of not being able to get out. Even if he had flames all around him, the pilot pledged to himself to let that rear gunner know that he was leaving the plane.

The gunners had no control of the plane and no control of the pilot's decision to jump. There was no warning device. If a gunner was manning his guns he'd be facing backwards and might not even see the pilot go.

Before a mission, Ensign Charles Draper and gunner Leo P. McGovern chuckle over the prospects of delivering a 1,000 lb high explosive device to the Japanese. USN via P. O. McGovern

During the dive the rear gunner had almost no chance to escape if the plane were hit. It takes a brave man to stick his head into the lion's mouth daily and then wait to see if the enemy will twist the lion's tail this time.

This was October 13, 1944, and the second day over Formosa. Charlie Draper was my wingman and his gunner was Leo P. McGovern. Draper was a good man to fly with. He had a round face and a sturdy build. He was a steady guy, a rock. You could count on him, and McGovern and I did.

Our target was a large, strategic, heavily defended airfield and air base on the flatlands on the western side of Formosa. The base was 1½ miles from the shores of the Formosa Strait, the 90 miles of water that separated Formosa from China.

Like all of us, while flying, Draper wore an aviator's summer-weight helmet, which was made of khaki cloth. His helmet being the worse for wear, he had just the day before exchanged it for a new one.

To protect our foreheads from sunburn, the helmets were cut with extra material across the forehead. When you requisitioned your new helmet, you took scissors, trimmed the part over your forehead to your eyebrow level and thus personalized the headgear. Then you attached your goggles, earphones and football-type chin cup, which made you ready for business.

Draper performed this little ritual but apparently did not pull the helmet fully down over his head when he measured to the eyebrows and chopped off the excess cloth. There was some slack in the top of his helmet.

That day over Formosa we climbed to 15,000 feet to surmount the mountains and make our attack. We came in from the east. The day was beautiful and clear, and as I peered to the west, way out, right at the horizon line, I thought I could see low-lying land, the shores of China. Just looking at what might be China sent a butterfly fluttering through my stomach. I knew then I was a long way from home. You've been as far west as you can go when you finally behold the east coast of China.

A strong east wind had piled up the clouds against the eastern slopes of the mountains of Formosa and high winds were sweeping down the western slope but this slope was cloudless, clear and in the bright sunlight. The flatland, beyond the mountains, was beautifully tilled and planted. The hedgerows followed natural contours, the rice paddies and the fields were irregular, but all were a full, fresh green color.

The big, brown-colored air base dominated the landscape, with its long runways and revetments all over, many with planes parked in them. There were big hangars and there were fabricated metal buildings containing, we had been informed, shops and warehouses.

As we approached the field the heavier AA began firing from locations all around the base. Our formation undulated through the sky—up, over, left, down, right, all in an attempt to throw off the marksmen below. As we neared the pushover point, I tightened my harnesses and made ready for the dive.

Later I learned of Leo McGovern and Charlie Draper's dive. They were the fifth plane to dive that morning. During the attack on Kiirun Harbor the day before, Jap fighters had been everywhere. Then, as McGovern and Draper had started their dive, the Jap fighters had joined right in, trying to shoot them down. This day, as the day before, McGovern had his hatch open, his gun cover pumped down and out of the way, his twin 30 caliber machine guns up and locked, and his armor plates swung into position in front of him and locked. He was buttoned in and ready. Given a chance, he would give a good account of himself.

As McGovern and Drayer reached the dive point Draper wrapped the plane into a steep wingover, passing from level flight, up and over to a 90 degree vertical "knife-edge" bank, and on to fully inverted. He maintained the back pressure on the control, bringing the nose almost straight down, aiming toward the air base. He rolled right-side-up in the dive and looked for his target. He had the whole airfield and all its buildings laid out before him. He picked a cluster of steel buildings that looked like what he had been told, at the briefings, were repair or machine shops, and made his bid to deny the Japanese the use of those buildings forever.

As Draper reached the midpoint of his dive, he was having great difficulty in holding his sight where he aimed. The wind that was sweeping down from the mountains, in gale force, in the bright sunshine, was blowing him off the target faster than he was correcting for it. He slipped and skidded and turned and twisted trying to stay on his target. The lower he went the more the wind velocity increased, a tremendous flowing river of wind disrupting his aim and his bomb path.

As the altimeter unreeled downwards Draper added to his effort toward winning the war by commencing to strafe with his two 20 millimeter cannons. He hadn't brought those cannon shells all this way just to take them home again. He reached the bomb release point, and knowing the wind was carrying him off his target, he kicked rudder hard to throw the bomb in the upwind direction and hauled back on the stick to make his pullout and head for home.

But, as he pulled back on the control, the world went dark. He was fully conscious but he couldn't see anything. Something was over his eyes. He tried to reach his hand to his head and tear off the blinders but he couldn't.

Draper was in the middle of a high-g pullout, his arm weighed eight times its usual weight and his muscles wouldn't react properly. He had to keep pulling back on the stick to make sure he didn't fly into the ground. He had no idea if the nose was now above the horizon or where, but certainly his first effort was to get the nose pointed up again. He held the stick back a few seconds more, trying to wait a decent time to allow the nose to come up to the horizon line or above.

In truth, as Draper decided to relax the pressure, the plane was already climbing vertically, straight up. As the gs dropped off he grabbed at the cover over his eyes, and found his new helmet. He'd cut out too little of the extra material. He'd not had the helmet fully down over his head either and the g-forces of the pullout had forced the helmet tightly down over his head and over his eyes. He tugged and pushed, but it would not release easily. At this point, the airplane would no longer fly straight up and it stalled, fell over backwards, dropped like a stone and went into a violent tailspin.

As the plane spun back toward the earth a number of things happened. First, Draper pulled his helmet back off his eyes and could see again. Second, he realized that throughout his escapade, he had never let go of the trigger and he had been spraying cannon shells at the rate of 1,500 rounds per minute in every direction. His bullets must have sprayed the whole air base and it was lucky he hadn't shot down a substantial part of the US Navy that was diving along with him.

Third, McGovern had decided that the plane was out of control and he'd better jump. Obviously, it was in trouble when it pulled out and went straight up. Obviously, it was totally out of control when it fell back like a stone and went spinning toward the earth. There had been no word from the pilot. McGovern couldn't even see if Draper was shot or unconscious. He did the right thing: he tried to leave.

For a rear seat man getting out takes time—seconds, perhaps, but here a man's chances for life are measured in seconds, and not very many of them at that. McGovern had had his canopy open. He slammed his machine guns away from him and locked them in their secure position. He unlocked and pushed away the two armor plates that protected him. He unlocked his seat swivel and spun around to face forward. He undid his safety belt and shoulder harness and struggled in the whirling, spinning airplane to get his legs under him and on the seat so he could push off and out. He knew he must jump hard to avoid being struck by the huge tail and stabilizers. That part of the plane could so easily break his leg, tear his chute or smash his head and render him unconscious.

As McGovern managed to get his feet on the seat to jump, Charlie Draper regained command again. He booted right rudder to stop the left spin, he popped the stick forward so the air flowed smoothly over the wings, and he then came back on the stick in a smooth but hard and fast pullout. The effect was to slam McGovern back down into his seat. Not a moment too soon; in another 2 seconds, he'd have been gone.

Gone? Gone and worse! That same day, at that same Formosa, at a similar air base a few miles down the road, Lt. John Thvedt and his gunner, Fred McCreary, were hit pulling out of a dive. John's elevators and rudder controls were blown apart. He'd lost control. The plane gyrated wildly through the sky. John struggled with what he had left of the controls, and after an unbelievable ride, he brought the plane under control, but not in time. McCreary had bailed out.

He bailed out near the air base and was captured. He was held for eight months in conditions not fit for animals. He was not given the status of a loyal combatant. He was not accorded the prisoner's rights of the Geneva Convention and then he was executed June 19, 1945, only two months before the war ended.

You had to be some kind of a person to be a rear seat gunner.

Like Charlie Draper, I made my dive on that big air base. I picked the biggest hangar as my target. Like Draper, I couldn't believe the wind. I did everything I could to try to stay on the target but I couldn't. I dropped my bomb and looked back. I had missed the hangar by a mile. Damn!

Yesterday Jap fighters had been all over us as we pulled out. Today I was busy looking for the Jap fighters, trying to see what the bombs were doing to the field, looking for fighters, trying to find our other planes to join up with, looking for fighters.

We had pulled out heading west toward the water. I was almost there, then I was there. What a relief! I looked back and swore again. One of our Helldivers—I couldn't tell who was the pilot—now out over the water was streaming smoke, then spitting a lick of flame, then spewing flames out of the engine and back over the wings beside the cockpit. The bomber was only

1,200 feet up. The plane rolled sharply onto its back and then its nose dropped toward the water and then in a smooth, even, but sickening curve, still on its back, it plunged toward the water.

I shouted in my cockpit, "Parachutes, parachutes." I wanted to see them so badly.

Pop, there was one, the pilot. I yelled, "One," and thought, *Let there be two, let me see another.* But rear seat men need time—only seconds, but they need those seconds. This gunner didn't quite have the seconds. If only the pilot had been able to roll the tab forward a turn or two to prevent the nose from dropping so fast, the gunner might have made it, but there were flames in the cockpit, and time ran out.

There was a second chute! The gunner had been able to jump! I saw the chute blossom and open a few scant feet behind the plane just as the plane hit the water. I felt elated and then deflated. The splash of the plane engulfed the chute. The gunner must have hit the plane as it crashed into the water. He must have been injured or the chute must have become tangled in the plane as it sank. Could he be alive? I'd go find out, but I knew in my heart that he didn't make it.

The pilot in the first chute might have made a good landing, but in that turbulent, violent wind, unless he dropped free of his chute just before he hit the water he'd be dragged and drowned by the chute. If he did get free he wouldn't have a raft; his little one-seater would be gone with the chute and he couldn't survive without it. God, I'd hate to be down there, especially without a raft. I had no idea who the pilot was, but I had to go find that pilot and try to drop him my raft.

I screamed instructions into the intercom: "Brownie, get out our raft. We're going to drop it to those guys that just went in. Brownie, do you hear me?"

Struggling to get our raft out, my gunner, Walter Brown, paused long enough to grasp the mike and *clik-clik* acknowledgment. I marked the sight of the crash and tried not to take my eyes off the spot as we approached. I was afraid that if I overflew it and had to go around and come back, I might not find the spot or the men again. I flew big S-turns as I neared the crash site, using up a little time to allow Brownie to get out our raft. The wind was fierce, sweeping down from those 13,000 foot mountains at hurricane force. The surface of the water was solid whitecaps and breaking whitecaps were torn off and thrown in the air as spume and froth. The winds were over 60 miles per hour and could have been 70 or 80 miles per hour.

When I reached my estimate of the point of impact there was nothing. It had only taken me a minute to reach the spot but there was no sign of the men. I started to circle and then I saw their raft in the water. It must have been torn from their plane by the crash and was floating just awash, flat, fully open but not inflated. I circled again and once again. Nothing else was in the water. No parachutes, no men. I came back once more to the raft. It rippled and undulated with the waves, in the whitecaps and spume. It was totally empty, desolate, mute, tragic.

I cringed within then turned to the east to make my rendezvous and join the squadron for the perilous flight home. I recalled all too clearly that yesterday our own air group fighters had shot down forty-six planes along the route I had to fly.

I needed company, friendly company, badly. No-one was at the rendezvous point. No-one! I was alone again. Maybe I could find them and catch up. But where were they? I debated about using the radio. I knew I shouldn't break radio silence, but damn it, this was pretty important to me, sort of like life or death right now. I stopped the debate with myself and went on the air. No-one answered. No friendly voice, no word of encouragement, nothing like "We will make two 360 degree turns so you can catch us before the fighters get you."

Well, I really couldn't have expected it. As the saying went, "Shut up and die like an aviator."

At that moment, loud and clear in my headphones, I heard Gene Schumacher's voice. He was the one who felt I had saved him from the black twin-engine Jap fighters over Kiirun Harbor the day before. Today, he risked the captain's wrath by answering my call. For that, I'll be forever grateful to him.

The squadron's call sign was Lucky. I was Lucky Four. From Schumacher came "Lucky Four, we have left the rendezvous, we're heading over the mountains on the plotted course for Point Option. You'll have to come on alone. I wish you luck, Jack."

Once again, I needed luck badly, and once again, I was blessed with it. I started in toward the western shore and wonder of wonders a thin layer of clouds was streaming down the mountains. The layer was absolutely flat and only 25 feet thick—it was so thin you could almost see right through it—but it was cover. The layer was at 3,000 feet, with bright sunshine above. I decided to fly just under it, believing the bulk of the Jap fighters must be flying higher and for me to sit on top of it would allow every Jap within 15 miles to see me.

I moved to just below the cloud layer but then I realized that the island was full of enemy spotters and that they would report me and vector the fighters to me. There was no rational choice. I decided to split the difference by flying right in the middle of the layer.

Now I was sure that both the fighters on high and the Japs below could see me but perhaps not well. They might not realize I was American if they couldn't see my silhouette. I stayed in the middle of the cloud layer, trying to sneak along but knowing I wasn't hiding it all. I was grateful to the clouds but I felt very exposed. I was sure my big fat rudder stuck up out the top of the clouds most of the time.

I knew this was like ducking behind a telegraph pole to hide while the tough guy on the block walked past. Maybe it didn't help and I sure stuck out around the edges but I did the best with what I had.

I made it across the flatland, I made it over the mountains, I flew across 100 miles of ocean, alone. I found the carrier. I made a good landing.

I've never sweat blood but now I know what it feels like to do so.

Who was the pilot I risked so much to try to help? Back at the ship, I found out it was Ed Eisengrein, the pilot I had been angry at the day before over Formosa when he lost contact with the skipper's flight.

Chapter 11

The beast will
bring you home

Lt. Leif Larson firmly believed that every pilot who survived, at one time or another, owed his life to the characteristics and toughness of his aircraft and to the courage and skill of his wingmen or squadron mates.

Larson knew he had some good things going for him. First was the plane, the Helldiver, the SB2C, the Beast. He liked the Beast. It was big and it was fast and, yes, it was a little hard to get used to and, yes, it had too many hydraulic lines, but he'd flown most of the planes the Navy had and he liked it. It was tough, well armored and well armed, and he felt he could count on it to carry the mail and then bring him back.

Larson felt he knew wingmen too, and he knew he had two of the best. Ben Emge flew on his right and Don Freet on his left. Freet was tall and rangy, Emge, tall but with that solid look. Larson watched the two of them kidding each other as they entered the ready room. They obviously respected each other, he thought, and they worked as a team. Freet was talkative and had a theory on everything. Emge tended to be quiet. Certainly, he became animated at times, and Larson well knew that even if he were Emge's leader, if he goofed, he'd have to endure a few choice words of biting wit from him.

The LSO directs a Helldiver in for a landing. National Archives

On October 12, 1944, the USS *Intrepid* was standing off the northern end of the island of Formosa, arming, fueling, launching and retrieving planes at a furious pace and it was having some troubles. One trouble was that after each strike, the ship landed fewer planes than it had launched. Another trouble was that the Japs were determined to sink the ship that day!

Larson shook his head apprehensively as the word came down from the air plot that forty-five enemy aircraft were on the radar, all inbound for the carrier. The flight deck was a mad scramble to get planes loaded and up off the deck, and at the same time pass the ammunition to the ship's own guns. The hustle and intensity of the sailors at their work aroused the gremlin in Larson, and as they spun open his adrenaline valves, Larson could feel the tension flowing out into his body. He quickened his steps to the ready room for the preflight briefing.

Ben Emge listened attentively while Lt. Joe Purdy, the VB-18 Air Combat Intelligence Officer, completed the briefing for the next strike, which was to be against airfields in northern Formosa. Purdy made it clear: "You have to bomb those airfields and get the pressure off the ship!"

When the briefing ended, Emge motioned to Freet and then walked over to Larson for his special details for the strike and pullout. Larson said, "We'll pull out to the northwest so we don't go over the city—too much AA—and then we'll bend around to keep away from Kiirun Harbor. That's a deathtrap. I'll try to get out over the open sea as soon as possible. Got it?"

"Yes, sir," came from Freet, a nod from Emge.

Two hours later, high over the most heavily defended airdrome in Formosa, with antiaircraft exploding all around him, Emge watched Lt. Leif Larson waggle his wings; turn over the lead and, indeed, the keys to his life to Emge and Freet, his wingmen; and pull up, over and down to commence his dive-bomb run. Seconds later as another burst of AA rattled and shook his canopy, Emge rolled into his dive behind Larson and Freet followed.

Ben Emge did his job with cool professionalism, and the big air base lost its best hangar when his thousand-pounder crashed through its roof and blew it into charred wreckage. *Now*, Emge thought, *pull out and join up to the west away from the city and beyond the hills. There should be fewer guns there.* That was the plan. Where was Larson? Damn it, did he make it? Yes, there he was—but off to the right, veering left, then right. Something was very wrong! Larson hardly seemed to have control of his plane. Emge had seen that kind of flying before. Larson had been hit! He was probably groggy and dazed, but still running at high speed, hardly aware of where he was going. He was heading north toward the city and toward that cursed valley of the guns, the one leading into Kiirun Harbor. Emge swore, "God, not that way, Larson! We've lost enough planes there now." *Okay, Emge*, he told himself, *be a good wingman. Go with your section leader. You can't let him go alone, but Holy Christ, not right over the city!*

Zip! Zip! Zip-zip-zip!

Tracers! Get out of here now, try down low! Emge shoved the stick forward and zoomed right to the housetops. Less AA, but what a ride! He could see all the details of the tiled roofs. He looked into house windows. He could see the faces of the people in the yards and streets looking up at him. The people looked surprised and scared. Well, it was mutual, so was he; any higher heartbeat rate and he'd have adrenaline shock.

Emge roared across town, dodging telephone poles, and headed north through the valley. He could see the river ahead, and beyond that, the harbor. He burst out of the town and out over the water and down to the water level.

The hills rising behind the moored ships and the jammed warehouses at Kiirun were a ring of fire from the AA guns on the slopes and crests. He pushed his Helldiver lower and lower. The downwash from his propeller blast left a wake on the water behind him.

Tension tightened every muscle in his body to the vibration point. He saw the guns to his left. He glanced to his right and could hardly believe the turmoil in the water from the shells. There were splashes, richochets, lines of bullet splashes and huge individual fountains kicked up by shells from the larger guns. He marveled at the amount of AA that a plane could fly through and keep going. He glanced ahead. The harbor was widening out, the pressure was lessening and then his heart froze. Zeros! Four Japanese fighters at the harbor mouth, just waiting for him to clear the AA guns of the harbor to attack.

Emge looked around for Freet. He needed support. Freet was right there doing his best to catch up. Emge reduced his throttle slightly and Freet slid in beside him. Larson was off to the left, the Zeros were coming in from the right. Apparently they hadn't noticed Larson and were coming after Emge and Freet. Emge could see that Freet's gunner, Walter Farrow, had his guns up and locked and was straining to watch the fighters. He heard his own gunner, Doyle Emperley, call him on the intercom: "Can I shoot?" In a laconic understatement, Emge said, as if extending a polite invitation, "Any time." Emperley entered the fight.

As Don Freet pulled in beside Emge, he could see the Jap fighters lining up for their attack. Two planes were now to the right and two planes to the

Lt. Donald Wilson parked his Helldiver in a catwalk after losing his brakes to hostile fire. USN via Donald Wilson

left. They were ahead of and higher than the bombers and paralleling their course. Just as in practice, the Jap leader on the right waggled his wings and commenced a sinuous S-turn that would lead him to a firing point 45 degrees astern of Freet's aircraft. Freet picked up the intercom: "Pilot to gunner, first fighter coming in one o'clock high. It'll be a full-deflection shot, lead him plenty!"

Farrow's voice was calm and very serious.

"Aye, aye, sir, I'm ready."

As the Jap fighter started his run, Emge turned hard and led the two planes right toward the fighter. As the turn tightened, the fighter had to tighten his S-turn. Emge turned tighter. Freet could see the fighter, now practically flat on his back trying to twist onto the bombers. He couldn't make it and flashed past in a streaming dive and climbed back up on the left side of Freet and Emge.

Emge's maneuver had exposed his tail to the fighter on the left. That fighter had not anticipated this hard turn to the right, however, and had not started his firing run early enough. Emge turned back and tightened that fighter's turn, so he too came streaming by with only slight opportunity to fire.

The second fighter on the right, having observed the bomber's tactics, started his firing run much sooner, and there was no way Emge would be able to use the same tactic on this one. Emge turned back but it was obvious that the fighter would come in dead astern of the bombers for an easy, no-deflection shot. Although it wouldn't be all that easy, since the Jap would be looking into four machine guns. Freet squirmed in his seat. The four light machine guns of the two bombers were no match for the machine guns and automatic cannons of the fighter. However, Freet knew that in the psychological battle no fighter likes to be caught dead astern of a group of bombers, exposed to the combined power of their fast-firing machine guns spraying clouds of tracer almost as if from a water hose. It looked fierce!

The third Jap attacker no more than drew in range astern than, perceiving his peril, he fired a short burst and broke off, first down and away and then up on the other side of the formation and back up toward his original starting point.

The enemy fighters were now commencing their runs from opposite sides in succession. Emge's twisting and turning into them disrupted their runs to some extent and the threat of the rear gunners with their hoses of tracers kept the fighters from pressing too close astern. Freet watched the melee of diving, climbing, twisting aircraft, modified slightly by the bomber's continued pressure to work farther away from the shore and out in the open sea. Freet instinctively felt that a land-based Jap fighter's peace of mind, composure and inclination to stay and fight would diminish in direct proportion to his distance from land, especially if he thought he was being led toward a combat air patrol of F6F Hellcats. Freet didn't believe that such saviors were at hand, but he could believe that the Japanese might think Hellcats were even now approaching as the Zeros fought out to sea and into the realm of the Hellcats.

Don Freet frowned as he studied the pattern of the Japanese attacks: the high-up forward start, the S-turn down, the sharp pull-up on the opposite side of the bomber. That pull-up! Some of those recoveries were pretty close. He barked into the intercom to Farrow, "When this next Zero goes by, get your guns over on the other side of the plane fast, and see if you can get a shot at him as he pulls up past us."

The attacking fighter rolled into the first half of his turn; made the second half, firing throughout; dove down under the bomber; came up on the other side; rolled partway around to begin his climb back; and at that moment seemed to almost hang in the air. Farrow had swung his guns and was ready for him. As the fighter half rolled out of his recovery, Farrow centered his sight on the hanging airplane and clamped down on his trigger. He was right on.

Freet watched the fiery lines of tracers bite into the plane, then move forward on the fuselage and into the engine compartment. Immediately, smoke began to pour from the fighter, its nose dropped, it fell off on its right side and it plunged under Freet's aircraft toward the water. Seconds later it hit the surface with a tremendous splash. There was no parachute. Freet was jubilant; he grabbed the microphone: "Good shooting, Farrow, good shooting. Keep it up!"

After a few more minutes of this violent and somewhat unproductive activity, and having seen one of their number shot down, the Jap fighters pulled up and back as if to take stock of the situation.

Throughout the fight Freet had been trying to keep Larson's plane in view and had frequently spotted him low on the water out in front. While the fighters were pondering their next move, he located Larson again low down on the water ahead to the right. As he did so, the fighters also saw the lone bomber and started after it. Larson was running at high speed and it was going to be difficult for Freet and Emge to catch up with him. Freet watched in frustrated helplessness as the fighters, with their extra speed, closed in on Larson. Freet and Emge pushed their engines to the limit. Additionally, they had a little altitude to burn and Freet could see they were gaining.

The flak-damaged wing of a torpedo bomber. USN via Intrepid Museum

The fighters reached Larson first. The two wingmen split and pulled up on each side of Larson, but out of his gunner's range. The leader could not make a high-side run because Larson was low over the water, but when the Jap reached firing range, he swept across the track of Larson's plane, raking it from one side to the other with machine gun fire.

Larson's gunner was Glen Hanks. Freet saw Hanks fill the air with tracers as the Jap leader swept across. The leader lined up for another firing run but there was no returning fire. Hanks' tracers had stopped. Freet gritted his teeth. *They've hit the gunner! The bomber's a sitting duck! They'll shoot him down. The plane isn't even jinking. Larson must be wounded too badly to even defend himself.*

The fighter leader now swung directly astern of the bomber and, with Hanks no longer firing, sat there pumping everything he had right into the Helldiver at close range. Freet could see round after round pouring into the big dive-bomber. He waited for it to start to burn; he expected it to explode in flames, but still it flew on.

Freet could do nothing but grit his teeth and swear, but he was closing in. They were almost in range. He fired a long-range burst. No effect!

The Jap was alert and could see them coming, but stayed, tenaciously shooting at the bomber. Emge opened up too and with all that tracer in the air the fighter leader stopped shooting and wheeled to the right. Freet fired again, and to his intense satisfaction, saw three of his 20 millimeter shells explode on the tail and rear of the Jap's fuselage. But to his disappointment, the fighter did not even slow down as he pulled off to regroup with the two wingmen to assess the situation.

By this time the chase had taken the planes several more miles out to sea and had cost the Japs one fighter shot down and another with some bullet holes. Suddenly, as if a consensus had been reached, the three fighters flared up and away, and flew back toward the safety of Formosa and their air base. Freet could scarcely believe his eyes but gave thanks to his lucky stars anyway and turned his attention to Larson.

He flew up close and looked. There was real trouble. The entire length of the clear plastic greenhouse was bashed and broken by bullets. The pilot's canopy, which had been slid back over the greenhouse, had the clear plastic completely shot away. The instrument panel was a shambles. The dials of all the glass instruments had been shot out and the instruments dangled on wires. Oil and blood dripped off the panel. The armor plate behind Larson was spattered with bullet marks, any one of which could have been fatal except for that wonderful armor plate. The top left corner of the armor had been hit with a cannon shell and smashed off. Larson was bleeding steadily from his left shoulder, and glass and metal had cut his face, neck and other places. Blood and oil covered the front of his flight suit.

Larson's rear gunner, Hanks, appeared to be dead. He was sprawled over his machine guns, bleeding profusely and not moving. Freet could see that Larson was conscious and trying, with bulldog determination, to stay that way. Freet examined the bomber's tail. The elevators had been hit hard by the fighters' machine guns. In addition, a gaping two-foot wide hole had been blown by a much-larger-caliber antiaircraft shell explosion, probably in the dive-bomb run. No wonder Larson had been a little disoriented as he pulled out and flew over the city. It was a wonder he had had control, and apparently he didn't have much.

Larson was flying low over the water. Freet knew why: you bleed less down low where the atmospheric pressure is higher. It was time to be serious about finding the carrier. Freet was sure that none of them knew exactly where the ship was, and they were too low to get a homing signal. He climbed up to 5,000 feet where he picked up the homer from the ship and immediately radioed the course to Emge. They were 120 degrees off the course to the ship. Even without the Zeros, Larson could never have made it alone.

As they approached the ship, Emge radioed ahead, "Helldiver coming in—badly shot up, limited elevator control, pilot seriously wounded, gunner may be dead. Believe unable to make a second pass. Get him down the first time or we'll lose him."

The ship's air officer, a commander, came back with the suggestion of a water landing. Emge gave him a big, strong, firm "Negative," and said, "Doubtful crew can even evacuate the airplane. Cannot handle a raft."

Then in his most authoritative, I'll-take-no-nonsense voice, Ensign Emge ordered, "Clear your decks and take him aboard."

From the ship came, "Wilco."

Larson had no instruments to judge his speed and position. Emge instructed him by radio to fly right-hand formation on his airplane and he would lead him up to the ship, straight on in. They came into the groove, and because of the great difficulty Larson was having controlling his airplane, they were faster and higher than normal. However, the landing signal officer allowed for the problems and gave him the "cut" too soon, which was just right.

Freet watched Larson chop the throttle and try for the deck. The landing hook on the plane, almost like a human arm, reached out and grabbed an arresting wire. The plane lurched to a stop. Larson killed the engine, the big four-bladed propeller paddled to a stop, and the corpsmen swarmed over the plane to pull out Larson and Hanks, stop the bleeding and get them to sickbay.

Don Freet landed aboard and heard the good news. Hanks was not dead. He recovered and so did Larson. Hanks had been hit by ten bullets and pieces of shrapnel. Larson had been hit by twenty-two pieces of shrapnel. The flight surgeon took twelve pieces of shrapnel out of Larson's back and neck and left the rest in him because they were too close to arteries or nerves to remove.

Twenty days later Larson and Hanks were flying again. They weren't going to leave the war zone until every Jap they could reach was cleared from it.

Larson thanked his two wingmen profusely. He said, "Why did you guys come up and chase off those Japs? Hanks and I were just about to shoot them down."

Larson's plane was considered unrepairable and pushed overboard. Emge and Freet saw it go. Freet summed it up: "The Beast is a helluva horse."

Chapter 12

Prayer

The day was October 23, 1944. All operational battle fleets of the mighty Japanese Navy were underway. They were coming to sink every ship we had. They approached in a gigantic pinchers movement: a fleet from the north, a fleet from the south and a fleet at the center. The two largest battleships the world had ever seen were in that central force.

We, in the fleet carrier *Intrepid*, a part of Task Force 38.2, were stationed off the San Bernardino Strait, which was the main deep-water channel from the interior of the Philippines to the ocean.

The central Jap fleet was aimed right for that strait and we were at the exact center of the bull's eye. We were sure that we both expected a clashing, grinding battle of immense proportions and intensity in the morning. The tension for many aboard bordered on active jitters, but not for me.

I was in bed by 10:00 p.m., went to sleep promptly, and slept peacefully and well until reveille at 5:00 a.m. How could I do this? It hadn't always been that way. This time my confidence and serenity came from a little prayer and a lot of faith.

Early in October, the Protestant chaplain had held a service on the ship. Perhaps it was on a Sunday; I don't recall. We had little reason to keep track of the days of the week.

My attendance at the service was due to a combination of circumstances. I had the time, since there was no flying that day. And I had some inclination to attend, primarily because I was having some apprehension about the risks in my life-style and had a growing awareness that there was a good chance I would not return home, ever.

The service was not lengthy, the sermon was appropriate. The chaplain believed that we were all God's children and that God would listen to our prayers. He said that if you needed a format for your prayers, consider first thanking God for all your blessings, then asking him for whatever you wanted, then having faith that as the Father, he would answer your prayers. So I tried.

I had recited prayers when I was little, and later in church. Our family had gone to church mainly in the wintertime and usually on alternate Sundays. This was because one Sunday we went with Mom to church and the next Sunday we went with Dad to the gun club. Those prayers I had said didn't really reach me but I knew there was something to them because prayer did reach my mother. I had seen her gain strength and serenity from her prayers.

She had made faith clear to me but I hadn't realized what she had shown me until after that service on the carrier. It was a simple but great thing; you either believed or you didn't. You accepted God and you had faith and you could feel it. I felt this on the evening of October 23, 1944, and had comfort from the feeling that God would support me whatever my problems were.

There are times in all our lives when we can't rely on help from our families or help from the structure we've built around us. There are times that no matter who we are or what we have done in the past, none of that will help. So it was at war. The best pilots and the worst pilots were shot down on the same hop. All the skill of the best pilot didn't save him, nor could his mother or a million dollars in the bank. Most of us, even today, have to rely on something, and when there is nothing else, for some there is the strong support of God.

If you pray, what do you ask for? Can you ask that you'll be spared and get home in one piece? Not if you believe in one God. After all, the Japanese and the Germans are praying too and asking for the same type of consideration. I couldn't ask that I be spared to go on killing them and expect that wish to be granted, especially if they were asking God for just the opposite series of events. That wasn't a reasonable request. It would be made from selfishness or at least a self-centered outlook.

If all the people in the world were God's children, I felt I should pray for all of them, Japanese and Germans alike. But for what? The one thing I felt sure that I could ask for, for everyone, was that they'd all get to heaven. But I wasn't too sure about heaven and I didn't want to ask for something for everybody that I didn't know anything about.

So, to reduce the problem with my request, and feeling that I might not survive the next day and thus, of course, wanted to be deserving and not self-centered in the eyes of my Maker, I prayed that all men who would die in the battle tomorrow would be "taken care of."

I left the details to the Lord. I left it to him to spare all of us as much pain and agony as he could and to take those he took to a place of everlasting peace and shelter. I said I'd like to live longer but I recognized my privilege to live was no greater than my enemy's and I could accept his decision as long as I had the faith that he, like my father, would take care of me when he called me.

With such a short prayer for all persons, on every side, caught in this war, I had the serenity and confidence to sleep well the entire night of October 23, 1944, even though I knew that the next day I would participate in Armageddon.

It was only five days after the shipboard chaplain had dared us to try the power of prayer for ourselves when I first put him to the test. We'd had a few days of bombing airfields where we found no enemy fighters and not much antiaircraft, and—although everyday I picked up a hole, or two or three, from antiaircraft cannons—I was getting itchy for some more decisive targets. After all, you could see a ship blow up and feel that you had accomplished something definite and concrete. I guess many of us had the colossal ego to think that extra effort on our part would change the course and outcome of the war.

In late September, before the chaplain's challenge to us to test prayer, I'd dropped my bomb on a ratty-looking airstrip on Luzon, or maybe Okinawa. Then, seeing a motor launch in a river a couple miles away, I committed a cardinal sin. Instead of rendezvousing with my group I broke

F6F Hellcats prepare to launch off the Intrepid. National Archives

ranks and flew over to strafe the launch and then came back to the group. It was risky, it was utterly stupid and it accomplished no mission, but the adrenaline jag from the extra effort and risk had helped me feel more useful and thus better.

Now, after the chaplain's challenge, on this new day in early October, we were again going to strike an airfield, and since my short sortie against the launch had gone all right, I thought I'd try it again if I could find a decent target. The captain would be furious if he realized what I was doing, but still, I thought I'd like to try.

I debated with myself until the debate was stalled. I thought of the chaplain and decided to look for an answer in prayer. I prayed to God that he would give me some sign. Should I split off on my own or stay in close with the group? I knew if I split and a fighter caught me alone, he would simply kill me.

After praying, I looked around for a sign. There was none, so I sat back in my cockpit and waited, alert for any little thing that might be a sign. I didn't want to miss some tiny event if it happened. This was a beautiful sunny day, clear and bright with a few fluffy white clouds on the horizon. The blue of the sky and the white of the clouds contrasted with and complemented the fresh green fields and vegetation of Luzon below us. It was beautiful. The squadron droned on, the sturdy-looking bombers in Vs of three, flying close packed, only a few feet from each other.

The blue-black Hellcats, our escorts, flying in pairs, slid smoothly back and forth over and across our formation. I could see another flight from another ship a couple miles ahead of us. The planes were all very purposeful and menacing but also serene at that moment and with no indication of trouble.

I glanced to my left. The two fighters that were supposed to be there weren't. A touch of anticipation flickered through me. Then, a good way out, I saw a little flurry of airplanes. Something was happening! I stared for a moment, trying to comprehend, when 200 yards away, right from under my wing tip, a fighter pulled up into the start of a loop. As he reached the top he half rolled out, in an Immelmann, and the low but bright rays of the early morning sun hit his wing and reflected a brilliant, blinding flash of sunlight right into my eyes. And there I saw, painted in the middle of that shining silver wing, the blood-red Rising Sun, the emblem of Japan!

I was awed. I could never have missed that blinding flash and the blood-red sun. I had to believe what I was seeing—no-one had ever had a clearer answer to his or her prayer. It was overpowering. I stayed where I belonged. We bombed the stinking airfield, and on the way home, 134 aircraft, ours and theirs, were shot down around us.

But for that blinding flash of light, my luck and life would have terminated that day.

Chapter 13

The fine art of buzzing

Teaching CPT Secondary should have satisfied my desire for adventure and excitement, but it only sparked the desire to fly bigger, heavier, faster airplanes. It was like being given a taste of freedom then wanting more and more.

As an ultimate, I'd love to ride a rocket. I'd start out straight up. Then I'd wring it out, see what it could do. Then I'd bring it back to earth and roar across the world at treetop level, occasionally pulling straight up, doing a series of rolls. Then I'd flip over onto my back and head straight down again. Then I'd do a swooping pullout, climb into a high wingover and dive back to the ground again to buzz the world.

Pilots are insatiable buzzers. I buzzed everything that moved and hundreds of things that didn't. Part of this was showing off, but much wasn't. You buzz a remote, inanimate object not to show off but for the thrill, the adventure, the adrenaline kicks, the satisfaction of honing your skills while risking disasters. How close can I come to that rock cliff? Does it matter if I fly too close to the top of a tree and actually brush it? Go ahead, try it!

The first thing any good boy does is buzz his home. A line of tall poplar trees stood beside our house. I'd come barreling in, just over the trees, pull up in a steep climbing turn and look back. Mom would hear me and run outside to wave. She always waved differently than other people. She'd wave up, up, and as I came diving down for a second pass, I'd stay a little higher, just for Mom.

The second place to buzz, if you could sneak over there, was your girl friend's house. My girl lived at a lake. I flew right over the house. She came out to wave, and ran down to the shore and out on the dock. I turned and came back, heading right at the dock. She stopped in her tracks, turned around and ran back for the cottage. I still remember that as a successful buzz.

Apparently my girl's reaction was a deep-seated thing, common to many citizens. I was flying a yellow Stearman biplane based at Pensacola and, as usual, flew it just over the treetops to check on how people lived in rural South Georgia. Ahead was a small farm with a little tenant house at the far end of a cleared field. I flew over the edge of the field, dropped below treetop level and headed for the house. The lady inside heard the engine and ran to the door. When she reached the door and saw me coming right at her, she stopped in midstride and just dove back through the doorway. I hoped she had a strong heart.

There was always the Boys-in-the-Boat Buzz. This was no trouble, and on my very first pass, they took me seriously and quickly bailed out into the water. I only did that once. I really didn't need quite such a dramatic reaction, but I was appreciative of it.

As a group in the Navy, we buzzed every beach we saw. Beach Buzzing was risky, however. One day a couple of our squadron pilots buzzed a party on the beach that seemed a little long on girls in skimpy bathing suits. The boys found out, to their sorrow, that the squadron executive officer's wife had invited some of the squadron wives to the beach and the executive officer, this being his day off, had gone along to help. He wrote down the plane numbers and chewed up the pilots.

The Football Game Buzz was a thriller. I was flying a Dauntless dive-bomber out of Alameda. It was Saturday afternoon, and as we returned toward Alameda, we came upon a university stadium with a football game in progress. The stands were full, the ends of the stadium were open. This setup had B-U-Z-Z written all over it. I came in one end of the stadium, 50 feet over the goal post at full throttle. As I hit the first goal line, I started a slow roll, and I held it until we blasted out the other end of the stadium. After all, the public, especially the taxpayers, should have the opportunity to see their warbirds perform.

The best opportunity for us to have a Let-the-Public-See-the-Planes Buzz occurred on Navy Day in 1943, when some public relations hound talked an admiral into letting all the Navy in the area stage a demonstration of Naval air power for all San Francisco to see.

We were to make a mock attack on Alcatraz and then, somebody assumed, we'd all join up over the bay and go home. Not one plane in the fleet did that. We all dove on Alcatraz, but then en masse we hit San Francisco. I flew up Market Street below the building tops for a few blocks, and then made a knife-edged bank up a side street that angled off to the right. Everyone stopped to look and be thrilled—and then hopefully went out and bought more war bonds.

The only thing that marred my trip through the town was that when I pulled out of my dive over the bay and went way down, right down on the water, the warm moist air condensed into instant fog on my windshield and I couldn't see 1 foot in front of me. I had a moment of sheer panic, but slammed open my canopy and did San Franciso and Market Street looking out the sides of the cockpit.

If you could ever get a warbird back to your hometown field, few buzzes were more satisfactory than a Hometown Buzz. The first time I was able to fly something hot home, I had a big new Corsair, an F4U-4. I was so excited and puffed up that I could barely fit into the cockpit. I brought it in meekly enough, just circling the field and landing. Even so, it brought the local boys out to the fences to watch.

When it came time to leave, they wanted a show and of course so did I. I asked the tower for permission to make a low pass over the field as I left and permission was granted—with pleasure, I'm sure. However, I didn't tell them I was going to make the pass at ground level, upside-down. They loved it!

I decided to make another pass for them. I bent the Corsair around and up, and as I soared upwards over the field, there must have been six little Cubs circling the field at 600 feet in the landing pattern. I pulled up to 3,000 feet in a wingover and, inverted at the top of the wingover, I looked down through the top of my canopy at the field. I could see the Cubs in the air stretched out around the field. I tried to make a mental note of their locations to keep clear of them. Then down I came, right down through their pattern, never able to see any of them as I went; then soared the Corsair back up to 3,000 feet in a flaring, rolling wingover; and then down I screamed in another dive through Cub Country, into an inverted pass down the runway and good-bye.

The response to that buzz set a new record for complaints at the Rochester Airport. The Federal Aviation Administration (FAA) inspector, Otto Enderton, was also a lieutenant commander in the Naval Reserve and if anyone knew how to deal with problems like this, he did.

Enderton was one of the last of the old-time pilots. He had a large head, ruggedly handsome features and a big mustache, and he commanded respect. He'd been a barnstormer in ancient biplanes and had flown almost every type of airplane known to man.

I'd no sooner departed the field than all the local citizens who had been in the air around the field at the time, and others too, came in to complain to Enderton.

After the first irate citizen appeared, Enderton prepared a most official letter on FAA stationery, addressed to me, stating that I had participated in a serious violation of FAA rules and regulations and demanding an explanation of my failure to report the violation. He could have written my commanding officer—that would have been trouble for me and would surely have discouraged buzzing at Rochester—but he didn't; he wrote me personally.

The letter was written strongly enough to scare me, but more important, it completely mollified the local complainants. As they came in, Enderton showed them a copy of the letter and they went away praising his strong, prompt action. The truth was that Enderton had loved the show. He'd put on better in his time but mentally he was with me all the way in the cockpit of that Corsair.

I wrote him a note of apology, pointing out that I had had tower clearance for a low pass but not mentioning that I was upside-down, and neither my commanding officer nor I ever heard further about the incident.

The Wake-Up-the-Tower Buzz was always popular with pilots. Usually, it was only done by those who were leaving the area for good, since a return to the same field and tower delivered you for retribution and discipline.

My best Control Tower Buzz was at Grosse Isle Air Station near Detroit. We flew Helldivers. The field was an old one and the administration building with the control tower on top of it was built right close to the runway, perhaps 100 feet back.

I was a lieutenant junior grade, back from sea duty. I felt pretty relaxed and confident. Confident enough to buzz the tower and return to the same field—and, man, that's confidence. I really hadn't thought about buzzing the tower and the consequences, and even when the situation presented itself, I didn't think about the consequences—I just knew it was going to be pretty exciting.

I taxied up to the takeoff spot at the end of the Grosse Isle runway and ran through the checkoff list, was cleared for takeoff and opened the throttle wide. The plane surged ahead. I held it down until it hit 100 knots and then I came off the ground and immediately, almost before my right wheel came off the pavement, started a clearing right turn—a carrier takeoff.

I cleared the runway to the right, rolled level and was looking directly at the tower a half a field away. I still might not have buzzed the tower, but a nasty little gremlin sitting on my shoulder goaded me to do it, particularly since the tower was operated by three WAVES and one had been pretty bossy on the radio.

I could have gone left or right, or over the tower, but I was on my chosen track and they shouldn't have built the tower so close to the runway anyway. I was in no hurry to turn. I thought about the WAVES in the tower and considered that they didn't experience enough of the real excitement of the war and maybe they'd like an exciting story to tell their grandchildren, so I really began to concentrate on the buzz at hand.

This had to be a pretty exciting little event, something they could always remember. With great concern for their excitement and that of their grandchildren, I aimed the plane absolutely and directly for their glass-enclosed kingdom. As I approached the last 100 yards, I slid the plane half a wing length to the left, and as I roared by, I lifted the right wing to the vertical, cleared the tower in a knife-edge bank, leveled out again just past the tower and climbed away. The WAVES in the tower had a very good look at the bottom of a dive-bomber, 15 or 20 feet away.

In the last few seconds, while I could still see into the tower, I was delighted to glimpse that confusion reigned. Two of the ladies were taking violent evasive action, one going for the stairs, the other flat out on the floor. The third girl stood her ground, microphone clutched in her hand. Within the reverberations of my passing, she came on the air with so much outrage in her voice and language that I laughed out loud. She was a lady, though, and conveyed an unbelievable sense of anger without the use of a single swearword. I was impressed.

I was also impressed when I landed 1 hour later and a smart-looking sailor of the Shore Patrol in Navy blues with white belt, white arm band, white puttees and a forty-five automatic in a white holster met my plane at the ramp. He conveyed to me that my presence was requested immediately by some high-ranking officer. Naturally I accompanied him and naturally I faced a stern accounting, a review of my bad conduct, a lecture on safety, and a series of dire threats to my freedom and future.

I must say he did well, but he wasn't as impressive as the WAVE in the tower. Of course, he hadn't been in the tower at the time. I hope the WAVE has pleasure in telling her grandchildren how exciting a job in the tower can be.

Buzzing wasn't all bad, as it did help the people become excited about the war effort and it wasn't always illegal. We also did buzzing for combat training as part of our program.

We did a War Games Buzz with great success at Martha's Vineyard in 1945. A squadron of six PT boats was out on maneuvers. The boats were told to simulate absolute wartime conditions for the entire three-day experience and always to be ready for a surprise from the "enemy."

They weren't told that their command had arranged that on the second day out, they would anchor in a protected bay at the east end of

Martha's Vineyard and a squadron of twelve Corsairs would stage a mock attack on them at noon, while they were eating their lunch.

This we did with glee. We approached at 15,000 feet and dove right out of the sun at the boats. Two or three of the planes worked over each boat. We were in our second pass before they were able to reach their decks and guns. Planes were flying at them from every direction. We were so excited by our sneaky and successful tactics that it's a miracle we didn't run into each other over the boats. Their Training Command classified it as a great learning experience about the effectiveness of the element of surprise, the necessity for constant readiness and the frustration of a gunner trying to pick one target when three are coming at him from different directions and sweeping just over his head before he can even swing his guns around to meet the challenge.

Later we buzzed in the Philippines and over the troops landing at the Palaus. We buzzed Jap ships and Jap airfields. Those buzzes carried bullets and bombs to the enemy. A good buzzer has his useful side.

Chapter 14

Bounce drill

Field carrier landing practice, or bounce drill, was as much a part of our lives as breakfast, even though we didn't have it every day. This drill was never routine. No pilot can stand and watch six airplanes fly slowly around the field, hanging on their propellers, flying at less than their power-off stalling speed, and not be mesmerized. Every minute or so, as the next plane comes into the slot for landing, there is a climax. Is the incomer too high or too wide or both? Worse, is he too low, too slow and out of position? Just before the plane reaches the landing signal officer, the officer must make a decision and give the pilot a "wave-off" or a "cut." Either brings on climactic action.

With a wave-off, all stomachs tighten as the pilot bends on full power and the wretchedly slow aircraft struggles to keep from mushing into the ground. As the speed builds a few knots and the plane begins to move off with more assurance, the observer pilots on the ground noticeably relax.

If it is a cut, the pilot chops his throttle and the plane starts down like a brick, heading for a sort of controlled crash. The pilot has no options and no reserves left except the strength of his landing gear.

Just before the plane hits the deck, the pilot pulls back on the stick, and if the timing is perfect, the plane strikes the ground in a hard, jolting, three-point landing and every observer pilot again relaxes with the feeling that his mental concentration and body English have helped the pilot make the landing.

The rest of the show could be called a prelude to trouble. Trouble into which any miscalculation or goof will send you.

Twelve of us were assigned to fly to an outlying field near Jacksonville, Florida, in six Helldivers, for bounce drill. We met at the flight line and drew lots. I lost, and so sat in the rear seat for the ride to the field. Once there, I watched until my turn came. We switched off every eight or ten landings for 2 hours before returning to base.

The plane had four gasoline tanks. The normal procedure was to run one tank dry before starting another. As Grandpa Pettibone (the mythical advice-giving oldest Naval aviator alive) would say, only a Dumb Dilbert would try to come aboard a ship with 3 or 4 gallons left in each tank rather than 12 or 16 gallons in one tank. He'd never know at what minute one of the tanks holding 3 or 4 gallons would be sucked dry. It's a bad mistake to run out of gas near the ship but it would be really stupid if you still had 12 gallons spread around among the other three tanks.

Bounce drill was the exception. You just can't run a tank dry and have your engine lose all power during field carrier landings. You'd be down in the trees before you could switch tanks and get the engine going again.

On any long hop, planes run out of gasoline from draining the tanks dry, and even though a pilot is doing this intentionally, he gets a shot of adrenaline when the engine sputters and dies. The first few times it happens, he immediately drops the nose to maintain air speed, and as he drops down, he quickly switches the selector valve to draw on a new tank. The air pressure from the forward air speed keeps the propeller turning and the engine fuel pump pulls gasoline from the new tank; the engine starts with a roar and the pilot pulls back up alongside you.

A problem arises if you're flying in formation. If you lose power and go busting out the bottom to keep your air speed, you may very well bust right into another flight of the formation that was flying below you. So, if you run out of gas in a formation, you steel yourself to the shock of the engine quitting, pull your nose up to maintain your altitude and drop back, not down on someone else.

Pulling your nose up and sacrificing air speed when you lose an engine are the absolute opposites of the cardinal single-engine rule of "When an engine fails, keep your air speed up," but in formation, fight your instincts, don't drop down, trade speed for altitude. In bounce drill you don't have options. If you're hanging on your prop at 100 or 200 feet and the engine quits, you're in the trees before you can help yourself.

Now it was my turn to fly. My alternate rolled the bomber to a stop at the end of the runway, blasted his engine, swung around and taxied up to me at the line. He cut the engine, waved me over and pulled himself out of the plane. I climbed up on the wing and into the cockpit. I loved to fly and bounce drill added adventure, excitement and a sense of preparation for bigger things, like actually flying bombing missions from the deck of a carrier.

I buckled myself in, ran smartly through the checkoff list and then started the engine, with the feeling of a knight mounting his white horse.

The checkoff list included the instruction "Switch gasoline tank selector valve to a full tank." I was moving quickly but not carelessly, I thought. The first thing I did was to switch from left main, where the valve was set, to right main; but I didn't realize that the pilot who preceded me had just switched to the left main tank and it was full. In my eagerness, I had switched from the full left tank he'd selected back to an almost empty tank.

I started the engine; taxied out; checked instruments, magnetos and propeller control; and then, full of confidence and controlled excitement, put full power to the plane, rolled down the runway and pulled up into the realm of the airmen.

This was a bright sunshiny morning. I made three beautiful landings; everything was just right. I felt like singing out loud, from *Oklahoma*, "Oh, What a Beautiful Day."

I wasn't relaxed or goofing off, I was alert. I constantly checked my altitude (200 feet on the downwind leg, down to under 100 feet after turning the base leg) and air speed (just above power-off stalling speed on downwind, just below power-off stalling speed on base leg). Engine instruments? All in the green.

I checked the ground too. It was the scrub pine forest country of northern Florida. The trees grew solidly below me except that here and there was a small clearing and once I noticed a trail winding through the woods, made, perhaps, by hunters in swamp buggies.

Having nothing but trees under me turned my tension up a notch or two. If you have to fly single-engine near the ground, it's better to do it over open fields. A forced landing in the trees is certain disaster for the aircraft and usually for the pilot. However, my tension was normal for this type of flying. I knew my beautiful, powerful engine would never quit on its own, and I certainly wasn't going to stop it myself—but I did 4 minutes later.

After that third landing, I climbed straight ahead to 200 feet, throttled back to cruise power and turned toward the downwind leg. I dropped my wheels and flaps and was adjusting my throttle and prop when the engine quit cold—and I mean cold, dead.

The prop was still turning from air pressure against it, but the silence was deafening. As the phrase goes, "I was too scared to panic."

In $1/10$ second, I thought of five things that might have happened to the engine and things to do, none of which helped. In that same $1/10$ second, by shear reflex, I clutched for the gas tank selector valve, found it and switched to another tank—but with the awful feeling that this wasn't the trouble. I knew I'd switched tanks when I started the flight. I was sure I'd switched to a full tank, so switching tanks wouldn't help, nor could I think of anything else that would. My beautiful engine had failed me. Somehow, someway, it had lost all its wonderful power and now I was going to get it. This was it!

The plane was coming down and yet I had to push the nose farther down or stall and spin. The plane came down even faster. I only had 150 feet from where I had been to the tops of the trees and I would lose that in 20 seconds. My wheels were down, my flaps were partly down, I could only pick a tree and hit it. I looked ahead and on my most sacred honor I was just coming over the edge of a little clearing in the woods. Salvation! Maybe the clearing was 100 yards—short, but long enough for me to get my wheels on the ground and slow down before I hit the trees.

If only the ground were firm and not soft and swampy; that wet earth would catch my wheels and dump me on my back, and there would be no way I could dig down and climb out from under an upside-down plane in the mud. And what if it burned? I'd drown in the mud or burn in the cockpit.

I shuddered; my mind curdled at the thought. But another miracle! The hunter's trace I'd seen ran through the clearing right in front of my nose. The wheel tracks showed that they, at least, were on firm ground. I'd land on those tracks. Hallelujah!

But Lady Luck is perverse and I was getting too good a deal; she had another card to play, a bad one. As I dropped down over the edge of the trees in the clearing, ready to land on the hunter's tracks, I saw that the way was barred. Halfway across the clearing stood two young but sturdy pine trees, each about 25 feet tall with a trunk 10 to 12 inches in diameter, sturdy enough to sheer the wings off a dive-bomber and explode the gasoline in its wing tanks.

The hunter's trace led right between the trees. There was no time to turn aside and no place to go if I did. I hunched down in my cockpit and aimed for a perfect landing. I would touch down right at the trees, I would take them both together, hoping I would not be flung sideways and capsized by hitting one before the other.

I was as cool and precise as I have ever been. For an instant, I thought again of all the gasoline in my wing tanks. The trees would tear those tanks, the gasoline would explode in a huge ball of flame, an inferno that would envelop the whole plane. I didn't want to imagine the rest and flung that thought from my mind. *Just stay in there*, I thought, *just keep solving the problems as fast as you can.*

I was 100 feet from the trees and flaring out for the landing, then 75 feet from the trees and 5 feet over the ground. At 50 feet from the trees, I felt for the ground with my tail wheel. In time, I was less than 1 second from the trees and disaster. At that moment an explosion occurred. Completely unexpected and out of nowhere, my beautiful big engine exploded into roaring, throbbing life! Gasoline, from the full tank I had switched to by reflex, had reached the engine.

Full power in an instant! I hauled back on the stick and bent the nose up 30 degrees in an impossible climb, but the plane zoomed unbelievably upwards the 25 feet to the top of the trees, and then at the point of stall, dropped back toward the earth on the other side of the trees.

As if my plane were a good horse, after I pulled it into the zoom over the trees, I gave it its head and let the nose down. I could feel the power but was it enough to keep us from mushing into the ground on this side of the trees? We did it. The power was there, the mushing stopped, and the plane steadied and picked up air speed, only 5 feet off the ground.

But now I was still down in the clearing and approaching the wall of trees at its end. This was the ultimate and final hazard. I needed only yards to get speed to clear the trees but could we do it? We were at the end of the clearing. I pulled back and the plane soared, not high, but up and over the trees in a wonderful, strong, climbing surge. It was music to my heart. It was more than music to my heart—it was my life returned to me once more.

Chapter 15

Coron Bay

The Palawan is a narrow finger of an island 200 miles long, remote and primitive, an island of mystery and of the Orient. It lies along the ocean road from Mindoro in the Philippines to the unexplored and wild jungles of Borneo. It is west of the Pacific, and west of the Philippines. It separates the South China Sea from the Sulu Sea.

As you fly north from the Palawan toward Mindoro and Manila you come to the Calamian Islands. We came there one day and left a quarter of our planes there forever.

The Calamian Islands are ancient mountaintops built up from the floor of the ocean. They are full of inlets, bays and protective coves, many of them so deep that ships often moored to the shore. The channels between the islands are deep but narrow and in these islands the Japanese captains felt secure from our submarines.

They also felt secure from our carrier planes. The carriers cruised the eastern side of the Philippines. The Calamians were almost 400 miles west and across the Philippines. Japanese air power had long been dominant in the Philippines. How could we hit them there, the Japanese captains pondered. Our admirals pondered that same question and decided how we could.

Orders were cut for air groups from two fast carriers: "Prepare flights of twelve VB [dive-bombers] from each air group for a maximum-range strike to the Calamian Islands. Load external, auxiliary fuel tanks, on all aircraft. Arm for concentrated enemy merchant shipping. Expect to execute low-level attacks."

We did as we were bid. Low-level attacks are two-edged swords. You fly right at the ships, so low and so close that your bombs can't miss. The flip side is that gunners can't miss either. It's an easy shot for them. It requires no deflection, no leading by firing ahead of the plane. It says, "Hey, gunner, just pour your fire right at 'em. Keep it up. They'll pass just a few feet over your head. Don't panic and you'll knock 'em down. Just hope they fly at you one at a time so we can concentrate our fire."

A low-level attack would be foolhardy against a warship's guns; it's life threatening against cargo ships. They may not have many guns but you fly right into the muzzles of the ones they have.

The day of the strike began for me when a blue-denim-clad sailor of the duty watch stood by my bunk and said, "It's o four hundred hours, sir. You're scheduled for a predawn strike. There's coffee and sandwiches in the wardroom. Good luck today, sir."

My roommate and closest friend, Walt Madden, typically, popped out of his bunk and immediately said, "Come on, Jack, let's go."

102

He picked up his shaving kit and moved off quickly to the washroom. I climbed out of the upper bunk and followed. A few minutes, a cup of coffee and a sandwich later, we wound our way through the packed and loaded planes on the darkened hangar deck, then up the "ladder" (a Navy term for steep stairs) and into the pilot's ready room. The ready room was attached to the underside of the flight deck and it bubbled with activity and tension. We pulled our long khaki coverall flying suits over our long-sleeved and long-trousered uniforms. After all, this might be the day we went down and if we were lucky and lived we'd need those clothes for living in when we walked the jungle or tried to exist on a life raft.

After the flight suit came the orange Mae West, then our shoulder holsters, .38 revolvers and cartridges. We each hung a long knife from our belts and then donned our gray-green air-sea rescue survival backpacks and parachute harnesses. The parachutes, with their life raft seats, were already in the planes. The parachute risers of each chute ended in a 2 inch diameter steel ring, which protruded from the parachute pack. It was this ring to which we snapped our harnesses on sitting down in the cockpit.

As we finished suiting up, Ens. E. Ross Bunch came by. "Bunny" Bunch was one of Madden's wingmen—one third of his team. The team was not cohesive. Madden was demanding. He wanted perfection, a high degree of performance and mutual support from his two wingmen. Madden had a strong ego and a quick response to everything. He was at his best under fire or in difficult situations. He met challenges head-on and he had the brass and ability to prevail most frequently.

Bunch had courage and was as good a flyer as the rest of us, at least until he became overexcited and hyper. At these times his mercurial emotions reduced his judgment and thus the effectiveness and safety of Madden's team. Bunch could become so agitated that he literally hopped up and down and words piled out of his mouth running together and hard to understand. It didn't give you a feeling of confidence.

Some of Bunch's closest squadron mates teased and kidded him, partly because it was amusing that he became so excited, so easily, and partly to make him shape up and fly right. It may have been amusing to them, but it was a real problem for Madden when Bunch carried on the war in his own way, almost without regard for Madden's leadership. Madden worried aloud about Bunch's reliability and judgment. He could have tried to have Bunch transferred to another flight, but he didn't. He did his best to play the game with the cards that fate had dealt him—and he lost.

Bunch survived the war but ten years later died a most violent, tragic and unnecessary death—by his own hand.

Back on the *Intrepid*, we had a final briefing, we wrote our recognition signals and radio direction finding codes on our plotting boards, and then, at the bullhorn's harsh command of "Pilots, man your planes," Walt Madden and I climbed the last ladder together and stepped out onto the flight deck to go find our planes. I was the skipper's right-side wingman. I would be the second plane off. Madden was a full lieutenant and led the fourth three-plane section. He would be the ninth plane to leave the deck. As we parted among the massed bombers and fighters he slapped me on the shoulder and said, "Go get 'em, tiger."

Madden was the ninth plane off the deck that morning but he didn't return that night. I never saw Walt Madden again.

I found my dive-bomber on the deck, with the plane captain standing by. He was as solicitous as a mother. He took my 2 foot wide plotting board from me and helped me climb up the fuselage and onto the wing. He slid the plotting board almost respectfully into its slides under the instrument panel. The plotting board was our navigation instrument, having a circular slide rule on it and being covered with rotatable grids for compass headings and wind vectors. The top layer was transparent and the underlayer was a chart of the central Philippines with latitude and longitude grids all shown. I had laid out our courses for the day and plotted where we expected the ship to be 6 hours after takeoff when we returned. I wouldn't have taken off without my plotting board.

The plane captain checked that my parachute snaps were connected to my parachute risers, then gave me the thumbs-up signal and hopped off the wing.

On command we started our engines, and after a 5 minute warm-up and check-out, the flight deck crew, using hand signals and flashlights, moved the skipper into the takeoff position while I jockeyed jerkily to the second ready position. With a rush and a roar the skipper was off the deck and 12 seconds later I followed him.

Everything was black, black, black, ahead. I had enough tension for an aircrew of ten men. I hated not having a visual reference, I prayed for just a streak of light in the eastern sky to help me control the plane. After all, as I cleared the deck and fought the skittishness of the plane, I was flying at or below power-off stalling speed; my wheels were down; I had a maximum load of ammunition, two 500 pound bombs and extra gas; and I was only 50 feet off the water and in pitch blackness.

Flying instruments under these conditions tightens your gut. I brought the wheels up, raised the flaps slowly and gained a little altitude. The plane picked up speed and steadied.

Now, I thought, *if I can only find the skipper*. According to the plan he would climb to 1,000 feet, maintaining his takeoff heading for 8 minutes. This would allow the others to clear the deck and stabilize their planes as they climbed out toward their point of turn to make the rendezvous.

At the end of 8 minutes the skipper made a carefully controlled 30 degree bank U-turn and came back, heading 180 degrees from his takoff heading. At the key point, I started my 30 degree bank, 180 degree turn, intending to intercept him at his same course and speed at 1,000 feet. My 180 degree turn should end with me tucked in under his wing in tight formation. Each pilot behind me would do the same until all twelve were together. This could become an awful mess with bombers crossing each other helter-skelter but we had worked hard at night rendezvous and as I turned I picked up the skipper's red and green navigation lights coming back toward me.

Flying half by the instruments and half by visual reference is the textbook way to lose orientation, incur vertigo and dig a big hole in the ground with your plane. The only thing worse is to fly half instruments and half visual at night with no visual reference except the skipper's red navigation light approaching out of the darkness. To fly under these conditions my eyes had to sweep constantly between my flying instruments and the approaching plane. This was distracting and disorienting, flying by references, half-in and half-out of the cockpit.

My eye sweep of the skipper's plane slowed down. I had to fine-tune my course, speed and rate of closure with his airplane. A minute more and I could make out the big dark blob of his aircraft with its little navigation lights accentuating the farthest perimeters of the wings and tail. It was like looking at a constellation in the night sky and trying to imagine what outlines the ancients saw that they could discern the shape of a bear, a lion or Orion from those few perimeter stars.

I gingerly slid closer to the skipper's wing and then stopped about 10 feet from it. That was close enough under these conditions.

The blue flame from my engine exhausts now illuminated his blue-black airplane in an eerie, faint blue, neonlike glow. I could just make out his helmeted and goggled shape in the cockpit. He was giving me the thumbs-up sign. He was damn glad to have me safely parked beside him.

Now to get the rest of the hawks in. One by one with smooth professionalism ten more planes joined us. With twelve accounted for we turned west for our dawn rendezvous at the Philippine coast with our fighters and twelve more bombers from the other carrier. As dawn broke and day blossomed we were on our way at 12,000 feet, southwest, across the Philippines.

This was still Japanese territory.

I thought, *Put your head on a swivel, buster, and keep looking. There could be a Zero anywhere.*

Never was there a better time to apply the rule. Eternal vigilance is the price of liberty.

A cloud deck was below at 10,000 feet, with an occasional break, through which I caught glimpses of inland seas and jungle-covered islands.

I swiveled my glance to the left, taking in the captain's plane. His rear gunner was having conniptions, waving and gesticulating, and then, when he realized he had my undivided attention, he pointed with both arms to a spot over my shoulder. I snapped around to look. I had no idea what I might see but it must be a real surprise. It was!

I looked squarely into a black burst of antiaircraft fire and then another and another. Fortunately none were too close, but the later bursts indicated the gunners were correcting their aim in a hurry. Our flight made a sharp descending turn and then pulled back up in a flaring turn in the other direction to confuse the gunners.

A section of two fighters rolled over, nosed down and went diving through a break in the clouds to find out who was shooting at us. In another minute they broke radio silence to announce that a heavy cruiser and her escort were almost directly below us under the clouds.

This was too good a target not to go after. The twelve Helldivers of the other air group were ordered to find a break in the clouds and attack, which they did with great eagerness and butterflies in their stomachs. Twenty minutes later, they announced on the air that they had sunk the cruiser and were returning home. Our group was frustrated; the other group had received the nod to attack an important target, and now they were going home. What did we have to do to get luck like that?

As it turned out all we had to do was to keep going.

We proceeded to the southwest and as we left the western shore of Panay the lower cloud deck became thinner with more breaks and holes and finally disappeared altogether. By now we were approaching the

Japanese ships at Coron Bay at the start of our attack. USN

Calamian Islands and strained our eyes to see what the targets would be. Hallelujah, it was a bonanza. Some fifteen ships were anchored in two protected bays. The first bay was about ¾ mile across, ringed by low hills with the south side open to the main channel of the islands. There, right in the middle of that bay, right ahead of us, were eleven ships and an armed patrol craft. There was a huge oil tanker riding low in the water, chock-full of precious oil. There was a graceful liner, a troopship no doubt. There were eight cargo ships, bottoms that Japan must have for its war effort. There was another big oiler in the second bay.

I was exalted. Here was the sort of opportunity we had dreamed of. This was a chance to be tremendously effective, a chance to do all that we had trained to do and a chance to justify four years of preparation for this act of the drama.

The skipper put the formation in a shallow dive down toward 3,000 feet and proceeded across the wide mouth of Coron Bay, the anchorage of the ships. We were moving parallel with the ships and when at right angles we would turn 90 degrees and attack. It would be a low-level attack. The skipper would be first and alone, I would be second, the other wingman would be third.

Alone? The skipper was going to have to hit them alone! Crazy! He'd surely get shot down. But we'd always practiced going in one after the other in single file. That was expected. No! This was crazy! *Throw away the book, Jack. Go in with the skipper and hope the others follow fast. Let them have two, three or four planes to shoot at not just one to concentrate on.*

The skipper rocked his wings good-bye, pulled into a vertical right bank, poured on full throttle and started down for the ships. I broke the rules and turned immediately with him. In trying to stay with him I flew about 15 feet below and directly under him. He started to strafe and his spent cartridges streamed down and banged on my aircraft. At that

106

moment he opened the big bomb bay doors in the bottom of his fuselage and I found myself looking at two 500 pound bombs, which if they were dropped at that moment would end up in my engine or in the cockpit with me.

I quickly slid to one side and started my own attack on a high-riding cargo ship. I clamped down hard on the trigger and felt the power of the guns and the plane as part of me. I was scared. I hoped they didn't get me but all over me I had that sensation of being indestructible, of being the hunter, and of doing my job with courage and with little regard for the hail of bullets from the freighter's machine guns. How close things can be! One bullet hit the root of my propeller and ricocheted away. Three inches left or right and I would have had a hole in the vitals of my engine and probably a 350 mile paddle in my raft to get home or find friendly Philippine guerilla forces.

As I closed on the ship I ceased firing and concentrated intensely on the imponderables of aiming the bomb and timing the release and on mustering all the skill I had to sharpen my judgment and send the bomb into that ship. I had no time to strafe or jink if I were to get a hit. I was coming at the broadside of the ship, below masthead height. At the last second I pushed the bomb release and pulled up but I was too late to clear the masts! I shot through between them.

On low-level attacks our bomb fuses had 3 second delays from the time of impact to the explosion. We were so close to the target that but for the delay, the bombs would have blown us apart as they dropped into the target and exploded.

My first attack carried me over the low shoreline hills and right out of Coron Bay. I circled back looking for a target for my second bomb. There was the liner. It was near the entrance to the bay. It had been able to generate a little power and was beginning to move out of the bay. *Can't let her get away!* I banked and wheeled through the sky and came at her broadside. I could see her guns firing at me from the foredeck.

I returned the fire for a few seconds but stopped to concentrate on my bombing run. I came directly at the ship low on the water, bombs armed, bomb bay open. I flew directly at her middle until I couldn't miss. I touched the bomb release, hauled back on the stick, and soared up and over the ship. No time to look back. A freighter was right ahead of me. I put my ring sight on his water line, clamped down on the trigger of my two cannons and zoomed over the ship with everything going. As I cleared the ship and rolled to the right I could see that my bomb had exploded against the side of the liner and now, with power dying, the ship was turning to beach itself on the shore.

The sky seemed full of aircraft going back and forth over the ships in every direction. One of our dive-bombers was crossing the mouth of Coron Bay, heading for the open outer channel. The plane spewed smoke and flames from its engine as it struggled to stay aloft. The pilot still had control. Obviously, he was trying to fly as far as possible from the ships in the bay before he hit the water.

He was losing altitude grudgingly but coming down nevertheless. He was too low to jump. A minute later he could stay airborne no longer and smashed into the broad main channel with a tremendous splash. Even as the spray settled the pilot and gunner were climbing out on the wing and in a matter of seconds had their raft out and inflated.

I banked down and flew 30 feet over their heads. It was Ralph Beatle and his gunner, Ralph "Bud" Johnson. As I went over them, Beatle gave a quick, over-the-shoulder wave of acknowledgment, almost without pausing in his effort to get the raft moving from the scene. His wave showed me that at least they weren't injured. As I pulled up two other bombers zoomed low over the raft, then we all turned back toward our rendezvous. We could do nothing more for them except to sweat them toward friendly hands.

Where was the skipper? I was supposed to be on his wing or close to it. I slid off south of Coron Bay, to our rendezvous point. A plane was circling there—the skipper. I joined up and others followed. Nine of the twelve appeared. Beatle was down; we had seen that. Two others were missing.

As we circled at the rendezvous point we could see a towering cloud of billowing, rolling, roiling black smoke rising from the next bay west of Coron. At the base of the smoke column we could see bright orange and yellow waves of flames, at times 200 and 300 feet tall, the whole thing boiling and seething like a cauldron of hell.

What ships were those? Who hit them? Were they connected to our missing planes?

We were at the end of our range. We couldn't go investigate; we could wait no longer to go home and we departed to look for our carrier.

Now I realized that Walt Madden and his wingman, Bunny Bunch, were the two missing pilots. What had they done? I could guess. As we had approached the first attack point, Madden had seen the second bay and its

After our attack, four ships burn in the bay. The plume of smoke at left is from the tanker that Walt Madden and his wingmen attacked. Madden and his gunner, Frank Crevoisier, were killed in the attack. USN

ships. He had seen the second big loaded tanker. Here was a target worthy of the best in us. Feisty Madden marked it for his own. He let the skipper peel off on his own attack, he let the others follow, he waved "Come on, follow me" to his wingmen, and he set his course for the second bay and the big tanker 3 miles away.

Months later we were told the final story by the wingman who returned to the ship. Madden did split with the rest of the flight. He made the choice between the relative safety of numbers in the main flight or his intense determination to strike every blow he could to win the war. He wasn't going to let that tanker go. He considered the consequences of his attack to the enemy but not the consequences to himself. In Roman times he would have stood with Horatio at the bridge.

As Madden's three planes approached the point of attack they shifted from the V to an echelon of three, in line to the left. This way they could see the targets lying off to Madden's right. They charged their guns, they armed their bombs, they opened their bomb bays and they firewalled their throttles. At the pushover point, Madden broke right to start the battle. Next in line was Bunch. Did Bunch hesitate? Did he wait a few seconds to establish a safe interval as we did in practice? Did he fail to see the need for a concentrated attack? If he did, he may have signed Madden's death warrant.

Madden's own aggressiveness had put his death warrant on the table. A good solid attack by three planes at once might have commuted it, but if Madden didn't get that support, the odds against him multiplied. Bunch did hesitate, how much we don't know, but after Madden made his 90 degree turn to start his attack, he was pulling away from Bunch at a quarter mile every 3½ seconds. If Bunch hesitated six seconds to establish an interval, then Madden, way out in front, alone, with every ship concentrating its fire on him, was a goner, and in truth, before he ever reached the ships, they shot him from the sky. His wingmen saw him crash and die.

The second plane made it to the ships before it went down. The third plane made it to the oiler, slammed its bomb into the ship's side and then escaped. The cost was high, but the oiler was destroyed.

Bunch, the downed wingman, and his gunner, Ed Cunningham, survived and like Beatle and Johnson, were last seen paddling like furries toward a nearby island.

After days of travel and unbelievable adventures and escapes, the two parties, each unaware of the other, were able to make contact with friendly Philippine guerrillas who brought them together. Eventually, after more unimaginable events and trials, they all were rescued by the USS *Gunnell*, a submarine, only to find they had to stay in the sub for the rest of its combat mission. The four of them finally left the sub at Saipan and were flown to San Francisco. By extreme coincidence, they landed there about the same time as the *Intrepid*, with VB–18 aboard, pulled into the dock. It was a great reunion.

The huge tanker burned until its steel plates were white-hot. The sea around the plates steamed and boiled.

A 2,000 foot high column of black smoke had risen in the sky. It marked the funeral pyre of one of Japan's few remaining big tankers and of the brave Japanese crews of the ten Japanese ships that sank there that day.

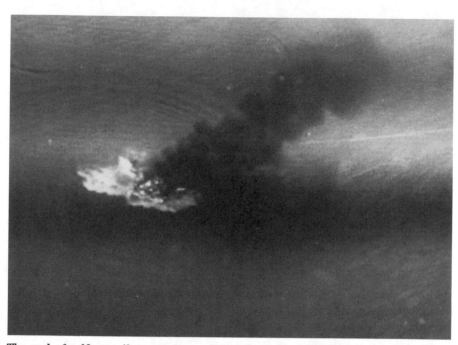

The end of a Navy pilot, gunner and dive-bomber. A Helldiver crashed seconds before this photo was taken. Its gasoline burns on the water. USN

The pyre also marked the final resting place of my friend, Walt Madden, and his gunner, Frank Crevoisier.

I arrived home from the war on Christmas Eve. Day of all days! The joy of my mother! Who could ever forget it?

Christmas Day I called to a distant city to Mrs. William S. Madden. Walt Madden was her only child. She had known he was missing in action, that's all.

"Jack, we watch the prisoner of war lists. Is there any chance?"

"No, Mrs. Madden, none."

A silence.

"In a letter Walt wrote that he had little confidence in the judgment of one of his wingmen. Jack, did that wingman let him down and cause his death?"

I thought of that wingman. Did he let Madden go in alone? I hesitated, I swallowed, I said,

"No, Mrs. Madden."

Chapter 16

Paddling to the Palawan

Ens. Ralph H. Beatle of Bombing Squadron 18 could have been described as a tall Texan, except for the fact that he grew up in Colorado. But Colorado or Texas, "Bug" Beatle as, naturally, he was called, was a good follower, a good leader and a clear thinker. He could usually be counted on to make the right decisions under fire, but he was having trouble today. He had just carried two 500 lb. bombs on his Helldiver some 350 miles in from the Pacific, across the Jap-held Philippines and then to Coron Bay.

As they approached Coron Bay, Lt. (junior grade) Victor E. "Tim" Serrell, the leader of Beatle's three-plane section pointed a gloved finger at Beatle and swung it from right to left. Responding smartly, Beatle dropped down ten feet, touched his left rudder pedal and slid left across the formation and up into a left echelon. From there Beatle could plainly see the targets—a bay full of ships. Two were tankers, both heavily loaded with oil; three were troop ships; nine were cargo carriers; and one was a Japanese Navy armed escort ship—all in and around the northeast corner of Coron Bay. The twelve Helldivers split up into three-plane sections, picked different ships and prepared to make low-level, mast-head-high attacks, exploding a 500 lb. bomb into every ship they could reach.

As they reached the pushover point, Serrell rocked his wings, made a flaring turn to the right and started down toward the ships. Beatle watched the second wingman go and then he, too, firewalled his throttle, rolled right, bent the nose down and started his bomb run. The first ship in the bay was a troop transport, a converted liner. Serrell was going for it and Beatle did too. He flew straight at it, came down to eighty feet over the water, bored into the ship at full throttle and released his first 500 pounder right at the ship's broadside. The bomb had a delayed action fuse. An instantaneous fuse would have detonated the bomb when it first hit water or ship right under the plane, and goodbye Beatle. But with a delayed fuse, the bomb went off deep under the ship. Beatle was clear and the ship, its back broken, was on its way to the bottom.

Beatle pulled up, skimmed over the ship's mast, and came around to pick his next target. Just beyond was a big freighter and near it, the Japanese escort ship. The patrol ship looked insignificant compared to the big merchantman but it was firing everything it had. Beatle knew it shouldn't be discounted, but he did anyway. He looked at the small warship, debating whether to sink it, then looked back at the huge ship ahead of him and opted for the big ship. He swung back around, made another wide-open low-level pass, threw his bomb into the side of the ship and pulled up, but not very far.

The feisty little warship got lucky and planted an exploding anti-aircraft shell right in Beatle's engine. There was no mistake. The smooth, roaring, powerful brute of an engine was through! It was winding down like a kid's toy and at that moment, Beatle knew he would not make it back to the carrier.

Beatle's first concern was to get as far away from his enemies in that bay as he could. He still had good speed and concentrated on converting every mile per hour of it to distance away from the bay.

The plane began to smoke heavily. It would be a water landing, and maybe a lot sooner than he hoped. He grabbed the intercom and yelled at Ralph "Bud" Johnson, his gunner, "Throw those machine guns over the side! Quick, we're going into the water."

Beatle had to get those guns over. They did lock in place, but he didn't trust the lock to hold in a crash landing. They could break loose and whip around, decapitating the gunner. In a few seconds Johnson shouted back, "Guns over the side, sir."

Now, how far could he stretch his glide? He couldn't. The smoke was turning to flame. He dove to get close to the surface, but he was far too fast to set it down. The flames started coming into his cockpit, burning around his shoes and lower legs. Still too much speed, but he had to set it down or burn with it. With a tremendous wrenching jolt and explosion of water, the plane hit and settled back, right side up, thank God. As the water from the splash cascaded around him, Beatle unlocked his safety belt and harness, and jumped out of the cockpit onto the wing. Johnson was out of his gunner's seat like a shot. He turned and grabbed the five-foot-long life raft container and wrestled it out onto the wing.

At that moment, a Helldiver, like a guardian angel, roared over them. Beatle glanced aloft. It was his section leader and good friend, Tim Serrell, trying to be sure he had survived the crash on the water. He waved his well being to the pilot and started again to help Johnson with the raft. Almost immediately, another Helldiver flew past. He glanced up again. The plane was very low and in a vertical bank. He looked right at the pilot. It was John Forsyth, also checking him out. A few moments of quiet ensued as he and Johnson inflated the raft while the plane sank further into the water. Beatle hopped onto the raft just as the plane slid into the deep and pulled Johnson aboard from the water. Two more dive-bombers flew over them. Beatle waved once to show he was alright and a second time telling them to go away and stop buzzing him. They couldn't help him anymore and he knew they barely had enough fuel to return to the ship. Moreover, he didn't want his friends calling the Japs' attention to his position and vulnerability. Nevertheless, when the planes formed up in the distance and departed, he had the ultimate lonely feeling in his gut.

There was no time for self-pity, though. They were about half a mile offshore and in plain sight of a number of the Jap ships they had just attacked and of a village on the island. They rowed like madmen for the nearest shore and the shelter of its jungle-covered slopes.

From what Beatle had seen, the island was five or ten miles long and fairly narrow. Somewhere, on the far side, there was a village. As Beatle rowed, he watched a variety of small boats and sampans running out and back, rescuing as many of the ships' crews as they could from the water and off the bombed and burning ships. Several of the small boats came within a quarter mile of the raft. It was obvious to Beatle that the Japs had seen him. They were exceedingly busy coping with the disaster the squadron had visited on them, but they would be coming to get him soon, and it wouldn't be pretty. If he let himself be captured, it would be a slow and terrible death.

They rowed even harder and in a few minutes the bow crunched up on the island shore, around the point and out of sight of the Japs. They deflated their raft, pulled it into the jungle and piled brush on it. Beatle picked out a landmark for their return and, to reconnoiter their situation, climbed the ridge that ran down the center of the island. As they neared the top, Beatle held up his hand, the hunter's signal to be quiet and not move. Beatle could hear voices and then a dog barked. Beatle motioned and they began a stealthy, quiet retreat back down the slope. Quite unexpectedly, Beatle stepped on a rock that gave way, and he came crashing down and rolled and slid ten or fifteen feet. The noise was so startling to both of them that they froze in fear. For a minute Beatle choked back the urge to run, and fought for composure. After all, where could they run to? The Japs were by now either after them or not. The two then pushed deep into thicket of tropical growth and waited for the Japs to come. They hoped darkness would get there first. The darkness arrived, but before that, the mosquitoes came. They bit unmercifully and rest was impossible.

Toward dark they arose and worked slowly and quietly down to the boat. Inflating it seemed to take forever, and by the time they were done, it was quite dark. To lighten that boat, Beatle ordered Johnson to leave the parachutes on the island but to bring along the plastic tarpaulins. The tarps were ocean blue on one side for hiding and yellow on the other side for visibility and rescue. There would be occasion to use both sides on the long and dangerous journey they had ahead of them.

It was now dark, time was racing by, the Japs were somewhere near and the insects were bloodthirsty. Beatle felt pressed and harried as they stumbled around in the dark trying to load and launch the boat. Once aboard, they manned the oars and headed southwest toward a string of islands in the Calamian group that would offer them cover as they worked down toward the Palawan. Beatle strained to recall every word of the pre-flight briefing about this area. Intelligence had said that he might find friendly Filipino guerrillas on the Palawan. He calculated that might be 300 miles away if they followed the shore, but he had no other choice.

They were no more than fifteen minutes out from the shore when Beatle began to think he had been pressured into a bad decision there on the beach. Those parachutes, or even some cutout sections of them, would be great mosquito and weather protection. The ropes would be useful everywhere, but he couldn't go back now. Or could he? Was *not* going back for the chutes compounding a bad decision made under pressure that he would regret later? He guessed it was but kept on.

They had to row across the mouth of the bay where ships were still burning. They expected that at any moment they would be intercepted. A cold wind came up, then it rained. The rubber boat was bulky, hard to row and impossible to keep on course. They paddled and rowed all night. At dawn, shivering, cold, tired, hungry and cross from the lack of sleep and the hard work, and with hand sores from the oars, they picked a landing spot and went ashore to rest. Beatle cursed aloud at the mosquitoes and to himself for not bringing a parachute canopy for protection from the bugs and the cold. At least, because of the night travel, they weren't sunburned, but something was the matter with his lower legs. His skin was tight and itchy or burning—burning? That was it! He was scorched by the fire in the plane and now was beginning to feel the effects of it.

By midafternoon Beatle was talking himself into traveling on, even if it was daylight. After all, there had been no enemy ships in sight all day and there seemed to be need to put miles between themselves and the scene of the battle. On receiving hesitant approval from Johnson, Beatle led the way to the rubber boat and they set out down the island chain.

Three days later, and considerably further from northeast Coron Bay, Johnson rowed them onto an island shore, where the cover of the jungle came down to the water. They landed and hid the boat.

Beatle's legs hurt. They were scratched from palmetto and thorns, covered with bug bites, waterlogged from the continued wetness, blistered from the fire and chafed by his flight suit. Some of the wounds had festered. He picked up his pack and walked to the water's edge and sat down where several big logs had blown down, substantially hiding his presence. He and Johnson sat there while Beatle bathed his lower legs. He heard a sound. A voice? He froze. It was a voice. Japs? Natives? Unfriendly? Friendly guerrillas? His pulse raced. He slowly raised his eyes, and there, directly in front of him—no more than fifty yards away—were two fierce-looking natives in a dugout canoe.

They had seen Beatle. They were looking right at him. Beatle said softly to Johnson, "Stand up slowly and walk slowly back into the jungle and then cover me. We may have to kill these guys. If they get me, you go on. One of us has to make it." Johnson rose slowly to his feet and walked into the jungle.

Beatle stood up slowly, consciously keeping his hand away from his gun and then raised his arms to horizontal and made the hands-down "come toward me" signal. The natives looked at each other and said a few words, unintelligible to Beatle, and pointed to a clear sand beach a short distance away. Beatle met them there and as they drew out on the beach, he could see there was something terribly wrong with the men. The man in the bow of the outrigger had gaping, open, festering sores all over his body. His nose was almost gone. One ear was gone. The ends of his fingers and toes were missing. Beatle thought he was going to throw up, but controlled it. These people were lepers. Naval Intelligence had briefed him that there was a leper colony on Culion Island, and this must be where they were. There had been no medicine for these people in more than three years. It was pathetic and revolting, but they were friendly.

The three sat on the beach, and with sign language, sand drawing, and a tiny bit of Spanish, they communicated. After a few minutes Beatle called to Johnson, "Hey, Bud, come on out and meet our new friends. Don't touch your gun, though."

The lepers told Beatle they had heard the bombs exploding at Coron Bay and were excited and happy to learn that it was the US Navy and that Jap ships were sunk. They were amazed that the Americans were there. The Japanese propaganda had the Japs invading the United States and fighting in California.

Beatle recognized their word for Japanese and then recognized their political persuasions when they accompanied the word for Japanese with an imaginary slice across the throat.

114

After a little while, the natives stepped back into their dugout and motioned the two airmen to follow in the rubber boat. As they rowed after the natives, they broke out the last of their Navy survival rations. About all they had left was a little pemican, which they ate to fortify them against what might come next.

The group paddled on down the coast and arrived at the leper colony. It was one of the most tragic places Beatle had ever visited, but they were friendly and the Japs wouldn't come near them, so they were safe for a while. The lepers did their best to make them feel at home and brought them boiled eggs and boiled rice served on banana leaves. It was no time to be squeamish and they ate the offering with thanks but not much gusto.

With sign language and broken English the headman of the colony made it clear that he would get a boat and a guide for Beatle and Johnson. Sure enough, three days later the jungle telegraph confirmed the arrangements. Beatle and Johnson were to meet a guide with a boat, about half-a-day's travel down the island.

Beatle gave the awkward and highly visible rubber boat to the lepers, one of whom would take Beatle and Johnson to the rendezvous in a dugout canoe.

As they walked down to the beach, the headman struggled to communicate their danger and some don'ts for their trip.

"Daylight, no go island to island. Japs see. Japs say, 'Spy.' Japs shoot. Ta! ta! ta! ta! ta! You go like fisherman—long shore. Be okay."

Beatle thanked the old man profusely, thinking how inadequate anything he could say was. There was no way he could repay these people, but perhaps he could help a little.

His Navy survival pack had sulfa powder in it. He had used some treating his legs and intended to save the rest, no telling how much he might need it in the future, but these people needed it so badly. They had been so friendly and anxious to help, and they were so pathetic. He reached into his kit and gave all he had to the headman. Then he and Johnson walked down to the dugout and started their long paddle.

For the next two hours Beatle, Johnson and the guide paddled along the shore. Occasionally, to save time, they ignored the chief's warning and took a shortcut from one point of land to the next point of land.

It was a sunny morning. The area was pristine, primitive, tropics. The shallows were full of birds and they could see colorful fish in the clear water around them. Occasionally, impressive looking sharks would swim by, eyeing them disdainfully as if considering them for their evening's main course.

Toward noon, as they were taking another shortcut across a bay, and were, Beatle estimated, a third of a mile offshore, the guide stopped dead still in mid-stroke and made a sharp hissing sound. Beatle had never heard that sound before, but there was no mistaking it. It meant just one thing—danger!

In the silence that followed Beatle strained his nerves, his eyes and his ears to detect the danger—nothing. Then he heard it. The faint rumble of an airplane engine in the distance. It grew more audible. Then they saw it—a dot in the distance, but coming their way.

The guide became very agitated, and made it clear to Beatle that they were too far offshore. The Jap plane would think them guerrillas and kill them. He dove overboard and re-appeared to hang on to the side of dugout.

Beatle needed a better answer. He and Johnson were still in their flight gear and obviously weren't natives. The pilot would be able to see them in the clear water. Beatle also remembered the sharks, a terrible way to die. "Bud, get out the tarpaulins. Get down in the bottom of the dugout, cover up and hope."

Beatle left a slit to peek through as the airplane approached. It was an old biplane but with a very real machine gun in the rear cockpit. As the plane started to circle them, the rear gunner swung his gun around and aimed right at the dugout. Beatle lay motionless and rigid under the blue tarp. He braced himself for the hail of bullets that would tear them apart and thought, "God, does it have to end like this?"

The guide in the water waved in his most friendly and hopeful manner as the plane circled closer and closer. It circled once, twice, three times, and then turned and flew right at the dugout, swooped low, and without firing a shot, left to finish its patrol.

Johnson pulled off the tarps. He was absolutely soaked in sweat. Beatle looked down at the sweat running down his own body and almost laughed in relief. The guide slid back into the canoe and all three paddled for the shallow water near the land. That was the last daylight travel for Beatle. Thereafter, they moved at night.

That afternoon they made a rendezvous on the beach with a man who would guide them down the islands to the Palawan and on to a guerrilla camp where they might have refuge. Obviously, their presence was known to the guerrillas. Beatle was forever surprised that every few days a man would emerge from a jungle trail or from around a point in a dugout and become their new guide for a trip through his territory. These people risked their lives for a handshake and in the hope that the Americans they helped would survive to fight again for the freedom of the Philippines.

About five days after meeting the first guerrilla guide, just as it was becoming light, Beatle, Johnson and a new guide paddled into a small bay where Beatle could see a rickety dock and on the shore a little hut made from palm fronds and bamboo poles, a "nepa" hut. They were welcomed into the hut by the owner, who indicated he would be their next guide. As they stretched out to sleep, Beatle thought, "What a luxury, just having a roof over your head."

Beatle was dead tired and felt he'd only been asleep for a minute when he was startled awake by someone pounding roughly on his back with his fists, and who, in a great state of agitation, was saying in Tagalog, Spanish and English at the same time, "Quick, quick, vamonos, vamonos, Japs, Japs, boat, Go! Come quick!"

Beatle was instantly awake and functioning. He could hear a diesel engine, a boat, and it was getting closer. Beatle grabbed his gear and followed Johnson and the guide out a rear widow of the hut and into the jungle. As they reached the cover of the jungle, he looked back to see the nose of a Japanese gunboat come around the point and head into the little cove. The engine sound was a putt, putt, putt—a noise that burned itself into Beatle's memory forever.

The gunboat was a menacing gray color and had an automatic gun mounted on its bow. Beatle could see three or four of the crew. The ship anchored and four of the crew picked up rifles and climbed into a dinghy. They rowed to the rickety dock and climbed out, their guns at the ready. The island was about a half mile long and a quarter mile wide. The Japanese patrol fanned out at one end and began a sweep down the island. They must know we're in the area, thought Beatle. His heart was beating like a trip hammer. It was so loud in his ears he wondered if the Japanese could hear it.

The guide knew his island well. He led Beatle and Johnson to the end of the island, opposite the Jap patrol, then worked into the jungle. Before long, Beatle could hear the patrol coming toward them. It was tough going through the brush. The guide listned intently to the sounds of the patrol, then motioned Beatle and Johnson to slowly and quietly follow him, and they took a few more steps into the jungle. Johnson whispered to Beatle, "Be careful, a slip now and we're dead."

Take a few steps, stop and listen, another few steps and listen.

Beatle felt a wave of relief as he realized from the noises that they had successfully slipped through the Japanese line and literally switched ends of the island with them. The guide was a master woodsman. There was no time for rejoicing. The patrol, rifles at the ready, was sweeping back over the island again. Again, the game of cat and mouse. Beatle thought of his deer hunting days, remembering how a big buck could, in the woods, sneak right through a whole line of hunters without detection. The thought was pure encouragement.

The guide led them along a faint trail on the island and as they passed through a very thick bit of undergrowth, a voice right at Beatle's elbow said in a husky whisper, "Take the left fork ahead." Beatle whirled toward the sound but could see no one. The guide smiled and motioned to go forward, and for the first time Beatle realized that there was at least one more guerrilla on the island, and he was helping the guide elude the Japs.

The patrol was thorough and determined. They seemed to know what they were looking for, and indeed they did. The Japs had put a price on Beatle's and Johnson's heads—$10,000 per man—and promised death to any Filipino who helped them. A Filipino informer was reporting Beatle's and Johnson's moves to the Japs. All that day they made more searches, and all that night they stayed in the area between the boat and the hut. The next morning they pulled up anchor and with that haunting putt, putt, putt, left the cove and moved off up the island chain. Beatle had his first sleep in 36 hours.

Weeks later Beatle learned that the informer had given the enemy a complete description and even Beatle's Navy ID number. Eventually, the name of the traitor was found out by the guerrillas. The traitor lived in the Japanese held city, Puerto Princesa, the capital of the Palawan. The guerrillas set up their own watch on the informer. One day he stepped out of the city far enough that his cries would not be heard and the guerrillas grabbed him.

They bound him in chains, wrists and ankles, and made him walk through the jungle to their camp. They tied him to a post in the broiling sun for two days and then killed him with a machete.

Linapacan Strait is ten to twelve miles wide at its narrowest, between Culion Island on the north and Linapacan Island on the south. It is a major seaway from the South China Sea into the Philippines and the waterways across them. The south half of the strait's width is cluttered with shoals and tiny islands.

A Filipino village was on the tip of Culion Island, on the north side of the strait. A week after the gunboat incident, Beatle, Johnson and the guide paddled their dugout onto the beach at that little village. The villagers turned out en masse to greet them. How they knew about his arrival, Beatle could only speculate. The mayor of the tiny town was most effusive, excited and helpful. He had already located a boat large enough to cross the strait and was assembling a crew of six good men for a couple of nights hence, who would paddle the aviators across the strait. It would take all night and be very dangerous, the strait was the main track for the Japanese ships. However, this was the last big hurdle to the Palawan with its friendly forces, and they would try it.

The appointed hour arrived, but nothing else did. After a few hours of waiting on a lonely, darkened beach, word drifted through that the crew felt the trip was too dangerous and would not be going. The mayor was incensed and set about finding a braver crew. Beatle was sympathetic. Why should these men risk their lives to return the two aviators? Maybe it was more reasonable from their viewpoint that Beatle stay with them for the duration, rather than take the risk of the journey. Nevertheless, in two more days the mayor had a new crew of volunteers and that night Beatle, Johnson and the six men set out.

At first the boat moved easily, but it was big, heavy and unwieldy. The wind increased and swung around to blow against them. It brought a drenching tropical squall, soaking them to the skin, and they shivered in the wind. The current in the strait increased as the wind changed direction and the rising waves made rowing difficult. Rain and waves filled the boat and they had to bail almost continuously. Their progress was slow. It began to appear that they might not make the southern shore before dawn.

As things became more precarious and the risk of discovery by Jap ships grew, Beatle's limited Spanish picked up some disquieting words from the crew and suddenly, he realized that the crew was agreeing that if the boat was discovered, the crew would kill the two airmen and throw their bodies overboard rather than be caught transporting them—which would be sure death for all. Beatle had the guts to realize it was probably the only thing to do.

This revelation made it imperative that they reach the shore before dawn. When Beatle took his turn at the oars, he made it clear to Johnson, who was also rowing, that they had a double interest in moving that boat toward Linapacan Island. Beatle prayed for a long dark night.

They didn't make it. Dawn came too soon and two enemy ships were visible on the horizon. One was leaving the strait, heading away from Beatle and into the South China Sea. The other was steaming east through the strait and in Beatle's direction. Beatle and the crew watched, eyes riveted to the ship in the distance as it proceeded toward them and rowed because their lives depended on it.

The ship's course would take it close enough for its crew to see Beatle's boat, and since there might be subs in the area and there were rocks and shoals in the strait, there would be lookouts all over the ship. Beatle knew his boat would be spotted. He waited for the ship to change course and come at them. Finally, they were less than a mile from Linapacan in an area full of rocks, shoals and little islands. Safe for now! No ship would venture into those waters. Sure enough, the ship rolled on through the strait without even a nod in their direction.

All hands bent to the oars and they made the shore, the bow sliding up on a sand beach in a small bay. The men sat back exhausted. Beatle had hardly taken a deep relaxed breath when armed men, with machine guns leveled, appeared out of the jungle and advanced toward them. Beatle's heart almost stopped. Was this it? He could feel his .38 revolver under his left arm. Dare he draw it now? How quick could he get it out? It was strapped in the holster. He'd be dead before he could free it. But wait! The men were all smiles, they were friendly guerrillas! They were men who had come to guide and protect him. To Beatle, these ragged irregulars looked like a company of US Marines coming to the rescue. Once again, he was among free and independent men; men with the will and the weapons to resist and to fight back; men who lived right under the noses of the Japanese and held areas the Japs didn't care to enter.

The guerrillas, Johnson and Beatle rested all day and at dusk set out for the main guerrilla camp on the Palawan, just south of Dumaran Island. The first part of the trip was by dugout, island to island, along the shore. On the third day, north of the village of Taytay, which was occupied by a Japanese garrison, the dugouts were pulled ashore and hidden and the party resumed its trek, traveling on faint trails through the jungle, and bypassed Taytay without a skirmish. With luck, the group would make the main camp near Mt. Lliam the next day.

Late the next day Beatle and Johnson walked into the guerrilla camp and were immediately overwhelmed by happy, shouting, cheering Filipinos. It was a hero's welcome and both Beatle and Johnson were a little abashed at the stir they had created.

The guerrillas were military people, trained by Americans. The headman was called Colonel. His word was law. The camp had been set up and supplied by Navy and Army forces. They had good things—jam and sugar and even some meat. To Beatle the new food was as enjoyable as a Thanksgiving dinner. As always, fish was the main part of the meal. Beatle learned that a Philippine guerrilla fishing rod was a hand grenade. When a grenade was tossed into a school of fish and detonated, everyone ate well for a couple of days. Another delicacy, when available, was wild pig.

Beatle hadn't been in the camp for an hour when one of the key lieutenants handed him a Thompson submachine gun and a half dozen grenades. He said, "Keep these with you at all times."

Beatle looked a little doubtful and said, "Are you expecting an attack?"

"We're always expecting one," said the lieutenant. "Surprise is our bag. We'll not let the Japs use it against us. By and large the Japs keep out of the jungle. We have the advantage here. When they do venture forth, we let them go out, but when they start back, we cut them off and kill all of them if we can. We also have ship watchers and relay messages on ship movements so the subs can get them. We try to know what the Japs are doing all the time and to always be ready for them."

The camp stayed ready twenty-four hours a day. Beatle could feel the wariness and tension; it was all pervasive. No one went unarmed.

Beatle and Johnson shared that pressure and had one more. They each had a price on their heads. It makes a difference. They slept on their guns, kept their backs toward a wall, and looked over their shoulders day and night. Beatle told Johnson, "Keep your gun ready and blast anyone who seems to be a threat," and he meant it.

The guerrillas frequently took prisoners to get information. The camp had room for only thirteen prisoners, and when it became full and another prisoner arrived, a prisoner would be tried and executed—it was just a fact of life. They couldn't be released and there was no room to keep them.

Beatle was present at the interrogation of a Japanese warrant officer pilot who had lost his way, landed on a beach and was captured. He was brutally beaten, summarily tried, convicted of the rape, torture and murder of Filipino nurses at Nichols Field, near Manila, and then beheaded with a Japanese sword.

These cruel and terrible deeds can be explained—but never justified— by comparison with the even more cruel and terrible deeds perpetrated by the Japanese on American and Filipino prisoners of war and civilians.

General MacArthur's forces had supplied this camp with four Filipino radio technicians and a battery powered two-way radio. To power the battery a Filipino hopped onto a bicycle hooked to a generator and pedaled like mad. Beatle was most eager to communicate, and particularly to discuss rescue. The radiomen advised that his presence had already been reported to Australia, who forwarded it to Washington, who sent it to Hawaii, who sent it to the *Intrepid*, which was now en route across the Pacific to San Francisco.

Radio contact was established with Australia, and Beatle took the mike to arrange a rescue. He was a little shocked to find that while headquarters would like very much to have him back, it wasn't about to launch a rescue mission at this time. "Sorry, Beatle, it's just too risky for you, for the Philippine guerrillas and for the Navy rescuers. If the situation changes, we'll call you."

One of the Filipino captains who had been standing by laughed as he saw Beatle's reaction. He said, "If you're going to be here for the duration, we'll make a soldier out of you. We're going to run a scouting mission late this afternoon. We'd like to have you come with us."

Beatle thought it over for a moment, decided he had better earn his keep and said, "Okay, I'm with you," and he became a guerrilla soldier for the next two days.

About four days after Beatle's arrival at the camp, a messenger brought news that two more American aviators were en route down the island chain in a sailboat from the leper colony. The boat was bringing rice to trade for salt. Beatle asked the guerrillas to do their best to have the airmen brought to this camp. A few days later, the guerrillas proudly escorted into camp Ens. F. Ross Bunch and his gunner, Edwin D. Cunningham, from Bombing 18. They had been shot down at the same time as Beatle.

Beatle was delighted to see Bunch—until Bunch announced that while they were both ensigns, he had joined a week earlier than Beatle and therefore was the senior officer and would take command from here on. Beatle couldn't believe what he was hearing. He said, "Look, Bunch, I don't give a good God damn about your serial numbers. I've been here working with these people. I have their confidence. We're making the plans. If you want to stay healthy and get back to the States, don't be giving orders around here."

The turf was staked out and it took Bunch only a couple of days to realize that Beatle was the headman in the Filipinos' eyes and that Bunch's survival might well depend on Beatle.

About the third day after Bunch arrived, one of the radiomen came to Beatle and said, "The Underground has made contact with the whole crew, six men, of a Navy four-engine B-24 bomber from Guadalcanal, who had bombed Puerto Princesa on the Palawan and sustained damage, which forced them down a few miles from the town."

"Can we get a message through to them?" asked Beatle.

"Yes."

"And bring them here?"

"Yes."

"Tell the aviators to get out of that area ASAP and come up to our camp where they'll be safer and at least ready for rescue. I understand there's a POW compound at Puerto Princesa and that many of the POWs are survivors of the Bataan Death March. Have you tried to rescue some of them and bring them up here to your camp?"

The Filipino looked straight at Beatle for a moment and said, "They won't come and we don't ask. The Japs have divided them into groups of ten, if even one man escapes, the other nine are killed. We tried it just once, never again."

A week later the six airmen walked into the camp and everyone celebrated their arrival. The new group was from Navy Patrol-Bombing Squadron 101 and included the squadron's skipper, Lt. Comdr. Justin A. Miller.

A war counsel was held and although the skipper of the B-24 Squadron was the senior officer, he recognized Beatle's rapport with the guerrillas and encouraged him to continue as headman for their dealings with the guerrillas.

The meeting over, Beatle went to the hut where the radio was located and established radio contact with Headquarters again. This time, with ten aviators to be rescued, he received a more encouraging response, and on a callback was told that two nights hence a PBY flying boat would land off the island to pick up the airmen. The airmen could hardly wait for darkness to fall on the second day. They gathered on the beach with their gear, lit a signal fire, and sat around straining their ears to hear the sound of those engines. They heard engines, all right, but it wasn't the PBY. The Japanese had also seen the fire and sent out an armed airplane to investigate. The watchers doused the fire and ran back into the jungle. The Japs stayed awhile and left. The PBY never came.

The next day Beatle re-established contact and was told that arrangements had been made for a submarine to pick up the group. He was given instructions to be at a certain point seven miles offshore at 10:00 the following night for contact with the sub. Beatle ran to the Colonel's hut with the news. He burst in and said, "We need a boat. A big boat. A sub is coming. He'll pick up all ten of us, but we have to meet him seven miles out tormorrow night! There're so many reefs and rocks, he can't get any closer."

The Colonel looked at him for a moment and said, "I'm sorry, we have no boat big enough. No can do."

Beatle was stunned. He couldn't believe what he was hearing. All this time, all this effort, and now a stymie. "Well, what do you have, Colonel? You must have something we can use."

"We have a boat half big enough, that's all."

Shook up all over again, Beatle called to the others and the whole group went down to the waterfront, where, hidden under the palm fronds, was a long but narrow dugout canoe. It was bigger than most that they had seen, but it shrank in size by the minute as they tried to envision loading in ten men, plus two guerrillas to sail it home, and taking that crew seven miles out to sea in the black of night. They tested it, all twelve climbed in, there were only four inches of freeboard amidship, too little to even be called a margin of safety, but in the end it was decided that it was a risk, but one that was well worth taking.

Beatle had no compass. How could they make their rendezvous? The pilots sat around on the sand considering every possibility. Without a compass, they had no way of sailing a course to the rendezvous, but if they could take bearings on two points on the shore, the rendezvous would be the point where the two bearing lines crossed. To begin with, they could use the lights of the camp on Dumaran Island for one bearing and the Filipinos agreed to keep a fire going in a small village about halfway up the hillside. This would give them their second point. To take the bearings, they made twelve straight ten-inch-long sticks and fastened them down on the stern deck of the dugout, radiating them outward in approximately ten-degree increments. They then laid out in the sand a model of the two lights and the rendezvous point and calculated what the bearings of the fires would be from the rendezvous point. With this crude pelorus, they were ready to make a try for it.

They next needed some signaling device. Their instructions had been to flash a light every ten seconds, but they had no flashlight or batteries. Their only source of light was palm buds dipped in coconut oil, which could be ignited to make a flare. The Japs would see those lights too. The Colonel said, "Maybe they'll think you're fisherman. The natives often fish at night on the shoals. But don't flash every ten seconds. That's clearly a signal."

Beatle thought to himself, "If we don't signal as directed, will the sub even let us approach?"

Night followed day, and the boat was pulled out of its hiding into the shallows and the men boarded. There wasn't room for everyone to paddle, but those that could did with a will.

The departure was most dramatic. All of the people of the village that were left, mainly women and children, came down to the shore and, as the aviators pushed off, the women and children broke into the song "God Bless America." It was completely unexpected and shocking emotionally to hear that song from those voices in this little Philippine village, a village that had been ravaged by the war. It was a ringing cry for peace, mercy and justice, and above all, hope.

As the boat pulled away from the shore, the people waved little handkerchief-like cloths—red, white and blue—and the singing swelled around the boat like a hymn as the children and mothers sang even stronger and more fervently.

As the boat continued away, the sound of the singing became fainter and fainter until it was almost ethereal, providing thoughts of home, honor, struggle and overwhelming empathy with the Filipinos who were suffering so much under the cruel heel of the Japanese.

As the clear children's voices reached out to him, emotion shuddered Beatle's whole body and his tears flowed. He glanced at Johnson who sat gripping the side of the boat, his knuckles white, as uncontrollable, blinding tears ran down his face.

After what seemed like hours of paddling and innumerable sightings by Beatle across his sticks to the lights of the Jap camp on one side and the fire near the village on the other side, Beatle issued the order to stop paddling and start watching in earnest. The horizon was divided into segments and each man was given a segment to watch for a signal light from the submarine. Beatle sat staring out over his segment. Twice he thought he saw lights and was about to speak, but decided it was a false alarm, his nerves. One more time he went back to check his bearings on the lights, and at that moment, Johnson said, "Light, a light. I see a light." It was on for a few seconds, then disappeared. Johnson lit his coconut oil flare, let it burn for about a minute and then extinguished it. No response. He lit it again in about ten minutes, let it burn for a minute and put it out. No response. He waited, then lit it a third time. The light on the horizon reappeared, and this time, sent a message in blinker. The message was "keep coming." They were right on line, but a mile short. Every man aboard grabbed a paddle and

A happy day! The USS Gunnel *has rescued 10 Navy airmen from deep in the Philippines. Six are from VPB–101 and four from VB–18. Five are pictured here. They are: Ens. E. R. Bunch (lower left); gunner Edward Cunningham (back row, far right); gunner Ralph A. Johnson (back row, third from right); Ens. Ralph H. Beatle (back row, sixth from right); Comdr. Justin Miller (back row, fourth from left). Note the special issue hats on the airmen.*

paddled like demons. In five minutes they lit another coconut oil flare and doused it after an answering flash from the sub, again with the blinker message, "keep coming."

None of them needed that extra encouragement. They churned the water with their paddles. They reached the sub and were hauled aboard by the sailors of the USS *Gunnel.*

It's a lifting, soaring, exhilarating, feeling to be rescued and tread again the friendly decks of a US Navy ship.

The submarines did all they could for the guerrillas. They brought out food, all they could spare, and they loaded the dugout with guns, ammunition, hand grenades and especially medicines of every type and supplies for the wounded and sick.

The rescued airmen exuded thankfulness and appreciation to their rescuers. They felt safe at last. But not so. The Captain of the sub, after welcoming them, said, "I'm sorry to inform you gentlemen, but your perils are not over. This is a submarine on patrol. We are outbound to engage the Japs wherever we can. You'll be with us for the rest of our combat cruise. You'll be seeing how the war looks from the under side. I hope none of you have claustrophobia and all of you have strong nerves. We welcome you aboard."

Fortunately, this patrol of the USS *Gunnel* ended fourteen days later at the newly liberated island of Saipan. The airmen were flown to Hawaii and debriefed on everything and anything they had seen and then put on a plane for San Francisco.

Beatle, Johnson, Bunch and Cunningham arrived in San Francisco on December 23, 1944, just one day after the *Intrepid* arrived there, and just in time to rejoin their squadron mates as they were packing to leave for Christmas at home.

It was a glorious moment to be home from the dead, and joyous affection—which never showed in the war zone—was in every voice and every heart.

Beatle, Johnson, Bunch and Cunningham were pummeled and hugged until they were bruised, but they loved every minute of it.

Then off for Christmas at home, shore leave, and to new bases to form new squadrons for return to the war.

Chapter 17

The message from Aparri

In October 1944, after two weeks of battles in the air, over the land and over the sea, the ships of Task Force 38.2 and related task forces pulled back from Formosa to prepare for sweeps against Luzon in the northern Philippines and later against the islands of the central Philippines. The big landings at Leyte would take place in less than a week and the Navy had to rule the air over the central Philippines by then. We'd go for the airfields first.

But now we needed to resupply and recharge the ships, their crews and the airmen. Relief for the airmen came quickest. As darkness fell and all the planes that would come back had come back, the aviators gathered in the ready rooms to find out what had happened to others that day. Each, of course, had his own story to tell, and it began:

"There I was, flat on my back at thirty thousand feet. . . ."

Each story gained and held the rapt but often raucous attention of the other pilots. No pilot can describe a flight without using both hands as planes, and wherever one looked at the ready room, wild tail chases or rolling dives with zooming pullouts were being demonstrated with facile gestures.

Each fast-carrier air group had a flight surgeon attached. Ours was a good doctor and a discerning man named John W. Fish. As the ships secured from battle stations and took up an easterly course, away from the scenes of battle, Dr. Fish appeared at the ready room door, followed by three able-bodied seamen, two carrying two cardboard boxes each and one carrying one.

The intriguing-looking boxes had familiar labels. In part the labels stated that each case contained forty-eight 2 ounce bottles of assorted scotch, bourbon and rye. Those cases also held gin, vodka and rum. This was a bonanza, like a dream I had had, as a small boy, of being let loose in a bakery.

The good doctor John W. Fish said in a most authoritative way, "As flight surgeon I am authorized to prescribe whiskey for each of you, which I do. Each man is entitled to two, two-ounce bottles."

As the discerning man Jack Fish said, "I now have other things to attend to. I will leave the whiskey in your care."

Dr. Fish stepped out of the ready room. The foxes were guarding the chicken coop and in 30 seconds the feathers were flying. I'm proud to say that every man drank to the doctor's health, and of course no-one that I saw had more than two bottles in his possession—at any one time.

Unfortunately, the toast to the doctor's health did no good. A month later, when the suicide attacks against us began, Dr. Fish was killed at his battle station.

The libation from Dr. Fish did its job, creating bedlam. It started slowly and then grew exponentially. In ½ hour the room was jumping with sweating, singing, shouting, swearing aviators in an effervescent explosion of their tension. Fortunately, explosions don't last long and in 1½ hours peace and quiet reigned again in the ready room. Two or three of the most boisterous pilots were sprawled over their seats sleeping soundly; the others had disappeared to dinner or their own sacks to nurse insipient hangovers.

A carrier is its own floating warehouse. It can stay at sea for months and contains most ammunitions and other expendables for fighting a war. However, three expendables must be replenished frequently. The first is oil (fuel). On the first day after our retirement, a huge fleet oiler pulled alongside as we traveled eastward at 15 knots. A sailor, by means of a handheld rifle, fired a light line to us. A heavy line was then attached to the light line and pulled to us. A very heavy line was next passed from ship to ship. Then the huge flexible oil hose was pulled to the carrier. Once it was connected the refueling process began.

The second expendable commodity is airplanes. These were transferred to us later the next day after we had anchored at Ulithi Atoll. They were swung aboard, one after the other, from a cargo lighter.

The third expendable came aboard late that afternoon. Ensigns, with their new Navy wings of shining gold, untouched by salt water, came aboard to replace our missing friends and roommates. Aircrew men, stepping smartly but self-consciously, came on our decks.

Oil, planes and airmen—the three expendables had been replenished. The ship was ready to fight again.

A day later we were underway and awoke to find the the sun rising dead astern of us. Our course to the west meant the fleet was looking for trouble and we found it shortly.

Every day as dawn comes the ships of the Navy go to battle stations. This is a dangerous time of day; the lighting conditions favor a submarine or air attack. Just before dawn a huge Klaxon will blast throughout the ship— "BRACK, BRACK, BRACK"—the bullhorn will then bellow "General quarters, general quarters. All hands to battle stations," creating an atmosphere charged with tension, action, hurry-up and urgency.

Men run through the gray steel passageways. The passageways are bisected every few yards by vaultlike steel doors. After the men pour through, the doors are dogged down with a dozen clamps to create waterproof compartments everywhere.

The ship echoes to the sound of hurrying, running feet and the slamming of steel doors and hatches being closed and bolted. The aviators and aircrew men reported to their ready rooms under the flight deck. This practice was stopped after a bomb went through the flight deck and exploded on the hangar deck just below the aircrew ready room, killing those who were in it. After that experience pilots were ordered to meet in the wardroom, which was just below the armored hangar deck instead of above it, and aircrews likewise met in their mess quarters below the armor deck.

126

A new Helldiver is hoisted aboard the Intrepid. *Aircraft were one of the three main expendables aboard a carrier in war. The other two were fuel and airmen.* USN via Intrepid Museum

As soon as this day was fully on us, the ship secured from general quarters and my squadron mates and I went down to the wardroom for breakfast. I walked down the passageway, toward the wardroom, behind Joe Purdy, the Air Combat Intelligence Officer. Purdy was 6 feet 5 inches and slender, with a bright red shock of hair on top of his head and freckles everywhere else. He was in his early thirties, an old man to the pilots. I said, "Hey, Joe, where are we going?"

"Well generally, we're suppose to clean the Jap airplanes out of the Philippines. There will be an invasion very soon and we're to control the air. We hit Okinawa, just south of Japan, and then Formosa. I suspect northern Luzon is next."

"What do they have up there?" I asked.

"Try two important airfields on the northern edge of Luzon. One is Laoag, and the other is Aparri. Those fields are essential way points for aircraft coming from points north all the way to Japan. They are essential not only to stage their attacks from, but also to hold their reserves and rearm their strike aircraft. I bet you'll be spending some of your time at beautiful downtown Aparri tomorrow."

"Joe, bombing airfields is not very satisfying. Even if you get a direct hit, they just bring out a lot of little men with shovels and throw the dirt back in a hole. Can't you do a little better for us? How about some nice, fat cargo ships?"

He grinned. "If you can find them, you can have them, but in the meantime, please help us win the war our way."

"Yes, Joe. Aparri, here we come."

And at midmorning the next day, I was on a hop, bound for Laoag and Aparri. But I never reached either of them.

The coast at the northern end of Luzon runs roughly east and west. The town of Aparri is about in the middle and the town of Laoag is on the western side. We flew in from the ocean to the east of Luzon at 15,000 feet. Bombers and fighters were there from three air groups. Comdr. William Ellis of our own Air Group 18 was the officer in control of the whole strike.

As we approached Aparri a VF-18 fighter pilot, Ensign Tracey, broke radio silence to report that an enemy float plane was about to take off from a bay that he could see through the clouds below us. "Permission requested to attack the float plane," came over the radio.

And from Commander Ellis, "Permission granted to you and your wingman. Rejoin us as soon as possible."

The two fighters rolled away and into ever-steepening dives until they disappeared through the breaks in the low cloud deck. As Tracey, the leader, burst through the hole in the cloud deck, the seaplane was in its takeoff run. The fighters zoomed down, right to the water surface. Tracey centered the float plane in his illuminated ringsight, touched the trigger and watched his tracers smother the target. The float plane jerked crazily to the left, burst into flames, hit the water and, with a tremendous geyser of spray, disintegrated. As Tracey pulled up and turned left, he saw another float plane anchored in the bay and for good measure destroyed that too.

Tracey then put on full power to rejoin the squadron. Just in case any Jap fighters were lurking nearby, he climbed at high speed at a low angle. To keep from running past and ahead of the formation, he made a wide swing to the north, and as he passed over the north shore of Luzon, at Camiguin Island, just off Aparri, he spotted four Japanese troop transports.

The transports were huddled in a little bay, right near the shore, trying to use the hills around the bay to thwart location from the air. They had made the passage down from Formosa in the night, and one more night would take them and the troops they carried to the central Philippines, where the soldiers would provide strong reinforcement to the forces there. These several thousand troops might make the vital difference; maybe with these men, the American landing could be repelled.

Tracey went on the radio: "Lucky Leader from Lucky 12, contact report. Four loaded troop transports at anchor in small bay on north shore. Position 120 degrees relative your present position and course, distance six miles. Over."

We all heard it and so did the gremlins inside me. They spun my adrenaline valve and the butterflies started fluttering. Four ships! At anchor! No armed escorts! Fully loaded! Wow!

Who'd get the nod to get them?

The nod was not long in coming. Lucky Leader sent the planes of the other two air groups off to Aparri and Laoag to bomb airfields and ordered us into action. We diverted to Camiguin Island just northeast of Aparri and there they were: big, fat, loaded, luscious targets, with practically no defenses. This would be a field day!

The first in were the dive-bombers. We came booming down, one after another, and every ship was hit repeatedly by 500 and 1,000 pound bombs. Then both the bombers and the fighters strafed again and again. The planes were over and around those ships like a swarm of bees. One ship had a little power up and beached itself, then lay there burning fiercely. Two other ships were burning and exploding from stem to stern. The fourth ship rolled over and sank within 10 minutes of the start of our attack.

Such incredibly good luck. Such great targets. All of them destroyed within 20 minutes and no losses on our side at all that I could see except three antiaircraft holes in my plane.

As we prepared to leave I took one more low pass over the scene and I wished I hadn't. For the first time I was aware that all four of the ships were transports—two were even converted passenger ships. The water around them was full of dark objects floating on the surface. Cargo? Yes, cargo. Men. Dead men, in life jackets. Dead men everywhere.

As I flared up and away I caught a view of the bow of a burning, exploding, sinking ship. The flames had engulfed the entire ship except for a small part of the bow and there at the tip of the bow was a small group of Japanese soldiers. I said to myself, *Japanese soldiers.* And then I thought, *No, not Japanese soldiers. Men. A group of men.* Men like me. Men with mothers and fathers, with sisters and wives. Men with little children, brave men, called to the cause of their country to give their all. Men who had been sent out and exposed without adequate ways to defend themselves, and slaughtered.

How many men? Were there 1,600 soldiers and sailors per ship? Maybe 6,000 plus men? Would twenty percent survive? I doubt it. Maybe 5,000 killed? Five thousand men killed in 20 minutes!

A crime!

A crime against humanity!

A crime I participated in! Awful!

But what else could I do?

Nothing!

Nothing else, nothing less, could deter them from their deadly pursuit of me and mine. They couldn't turn back, nor could I.

The road we both marched on was built in prior years by other men.

God, if those leaders could be here now to see, to feel, to experience this carnage.

Those leaders had to believe themselves to be good men who did their best.

The message from Aparri is clear: We have to do better! Now!

Chapter 18

Honest John Gilman

John S. Gilman graduated from Williams College in 1940. A year later, Pearl Harbor erupted, and shortly thereafter, he was US Naval aviation cadet Gilman. Gilman was tall and wiry, with a great head for figures and logic. He was straightforward and loyal to the core. His family had been distinguished lawyers and he had decided to carry on the tradition. His personal sense of honor and duty was so exceptional that at times, his friends had been known to call him Honest Abe.

In 1942, there was a war to be won and Gilman was at Melborne Beach, Florida, training to be a US Navy fighter pilot. A call went out for volunteers to form the Navy's first carrier-based nightfighter squadron. Gilman was quick to pick up the gauntlet and volunteered.

The training was intense, exciting and dangerous, but most of the first group did survive and were eventually assigned to the big carriers. That's why, on March 31, 1944, at 5:10 in the morning, in pitch darkness, Honest John Gilman was sitting in the cockpit of an F6F-N Hellcat nightfighter on the deck of the USS *Lexington*, about to be catapulted into the black void of the night to pursue a Japanese snooper.

The snooper was heading east from the Palau Islands. The fighter director officer in the high tower of the *Lexington*'s superstructure, radio mike in hand, was hunched over the radarscope with the radar men studying the green line sweeping around and around the scope. A dot was at the edge of the screen. Each sweep of the green line showed that the dot was moving steadily toward the center of the scope. This movement was of great interest to the intently watching officer and men because the center of the scope represented the *Lexington* herself.

The fighter director officer pressed his transmitter button and spoke directly to Gilman in the fighter: "Cobalt 7 from Base, we have a bogey at forty miles bearing 278 degrees. Stand by to launch. State your condition. Over."

Gilman answered, "Cobalt Base, Cobalt 7. Condition one, check list complete. Ready for takeoff when ordered. Over."

Two minutes later, the catapult officer gave Gilman the traditional thumbs-up signal, the pilot returned the signal, the catapult fired and the darkened, coal-black fighter was shot down the deck like a cannon ball into the black of the night. He was immediately lost from sight to the ship. But in the armored radar control center of the ship, a new green dot appeared on the screen, and under direction from the fighter director officer, it curved west, toward the intruder.

The nightfighter was a modified Grumman Hellcat with state-of-the-art instruments for night flying and radar interception. It had a built-in radar system that started with a radome, not quite 2 feet across, mounted way out on the right wing of the plane and ended in the cockpit with the pilot's own radarscope. The system had a limited range of about 4 miles.

The fighter director officer began to vector Cobalt 7 to bring it within 4 miles of the bogey so the pilot could pursue the quarry on his own radar.

The two blips began to close, when suddenly the bogey made a 180 degree turn to the west.

From the fighter director came, "Cobalt 7, Base. Bogey has reversed course to 285 degrees. Vector 280, buster."

Gilman responded, "Seven, roger."

Gilman put on maximum power and adjusted his heading to 280 degrees. Both planes were now headed west at high speed, with the night-fighter gaining gradually.

Unfortunately, neither the radar of the ship nor the radar of the aircraft had the capacity to determine the altitude of the intruder. Gilman attempted to search high, by pulling his plane's nose up, and low, by pointing it down, but he couldn't pick up the snooper. He tried again and again to make contact. Then the fighter director came on the air: "Cobalt 7, Base. The bogey has now disappeared from our screen. You are ordered to return to base. Fly vectors 095, Angels 10. Over."

"Roger, Base. Cobalt 7."

Gilman reversed his course and headed east where dawn had broken and light was spreading. With that light in the east, the snooper must have been able to see Cobalt 7 pursuing and had taken evasive action while Gilman, looking west, could see only darkness.

As Gilman headed home and the sky became lighter and lighter, he could see a formation of sixteen aircraft flying west. They would pass 2 miles to his north. This was the first fighter sweep of the day from our carriers and the planes were easily recognizable as Hellcats. Gilman thought, it will be a tough day for the Japs in the Palaus with flight after flight like that, to wreak havoc on their installations.

As he watched the approaching flight, one of the aircraft rolled up on its left wing and turned toward Gilman, turned right at him! Short of shooting, this was the most hostile thing a pilot could do. He was pointing six loaded machine guns right at Gilman and appeared to have every intention of using them. This overaggressive, eager ensign was trying to be a hero and shoot down his first Jap—but this wasn't a Jap, this was Honest John Gilman he was lining up to kill.

There was now enough daylight for a pilot to identify Gilman's F6F as a friendly Hellcat. None of the other fifteen pilots, which obviously could see him, was breaking off to join the attack. What was this idiot thinking about? Where were his brains?

Gilman had a few options. He could get on the radio and call the dog off, but the nightfighters were on one frequency and the fighter sweep was on another. They couldn't communicate. Damn!

He could turn broadside and show the jerk his profile. Everyone in the fleet, and the Japanese fleet for that matter, knew the profile of an F6F. But if this guy was as dumb and as oblivious as he was acting, it was a good bet that the profile would never register and Gilman would be a sitting duck to be shot down because the aggressor would end up on his tail. Gilman had no time for deliberations and he wasn't going to put his trust in the unthinking pilot and let him get on his tail.

He could also choose the instinctive option, which was to turn toward the aggressor and brazen it out with a head-on run. This would be short and sweet or short and bitter. He'd have to survive one firing pass to live.

For an instant, John Gilman was tempted to charge his guns with bullets and shoot first—but no, that was a US Navy plane and an American pilot coming at him. His loyalty and instincts were too deep to shoot at a friendly pilot, even if this meant he himself would be shot down or, and he couldn't visualize it, shot dead. Shooting down an American was too much for Gilman's conscience. He didn't charge his guns.

The planes came at each other head-on, full throttle, one intent upon the kill, the other trying desperately to avoid the unfolding tragedy.

The range was closing at 900 feet per second. What could Gilman do? The eager beaver would fire his six machine guns right at him, any split second now! The planes were lined up dead at each other. They would crash head-on!

Gilman waited a tiny fraction of a second longer. Just when he felt his assailant was at the firing point—and firing point or not, the planes would crash head-on if he didn't do something, NOW—he did something! He booted left rudder with all his strength. The plane jumped in response and slid left. At that very instant the attacker touched off his guns and fifty bullets per second tore into the nightfighter. The planes passed each other in a microsecond, missing by inches. Cobalt 7 was riddled, but because of his last-chance slide to the left, only the plane's right side was shattered and John Gilman still lived.

The radar dome, on the right wing, had been shot into a thousand pieces and had disappeared, leaving the leading edge of the wing with a 2 foot wide flat area facing forward—a tremendous drag. The end of the right wing was frayed and shredded, and the Pitot tube was gone, so Gilman would receive no air speed indication again. The tail had been hit, the rudder was jammed and locked, and the plane was in a right turn, and barely controllable.

Having a jammed, locked or unresponsive control is sheer terror for a pilot. The prospects of a crash are bad enough but locked controls are worse. The essence, the heart of flying is those controls—their responsiveness and their basic relationship to the whole of flying that plane—so that when you lose control this brings on the primeval scream, not usually uttered but felt from the soles of your feet to the top of your head. The whole system, the whole structure, the whole art and skill of flying are gone. You are left falling through space in an uncontrollable, unpredictable, unknown void. It penetrates like no other experience.

John Gilman felt as though a cold steel broadsword had been rammed through his stomach. He balanced on the lip of the precipice of sheer panic. He steadied himself. He wasn't dead yet. The plane was responding a little, but it was still in a right turn, dragging its shredded wing and ruined radome through the sky in a skidding, sideways motion.

Was he doomed to continue to circle where he was until he ran out of gas or spun in? A rudder would have made it easier. He looked around for help. His assailant had finally seen enough to recognize the terrible mistake he had made and had streaked after his flight and disappeared with them.

Honest John Gilman, who all his life had stood for fairness and help for his fellow men, could forgive a lot—even being shot at—but he could never forgive that pilot for leaving him, alone. His plane was badly shot up, he was barely able to control it and he could expect no help back to the ship or even a friendly escort to advise rescue forces where he went down, if he couldn't make it. He needed help. For the first time anger welled up in him. He spit out an oath and went back to flying his cripple.

Gilman gingerly experimented with the controls and found he had more than he at first thought. First and foremost he had his engine. That lovely brute up front was all there, putting out for him, steady and strong. Its very sturdiness, reliability and surging power gave him strength and steadiness. Pilots learn to love their engines.

He had his elevators, probably his most crucial control.

The rudder was frozen but that wasn't critical, he thought. It is well that he didn't think further; the rudder would become all-critical when it came time to land aboard. It was his last resort to prevent or control a spin.

He had no air speed indicator. That was critical! A cold shudder swept through him. You can't land aboard without air speed control. You'll be too fast and crash the barriers or, the unthinkable, you'll stall on the approach and spin in. People don't walk away from spinning straight in. Well, he had the alternative to land in the water but flying sideways as he was, could he do it? Could he do it and get out? He had to know his air speed.

The ailerons? They were responding but sluggish and sloppy. Using them he stopped the right turn and straightened the airplane out with the right wing high and the fuselage slipping somewhat sideways through the air. Did he have enough control to land aboard? He didn't know. The LSO would decide that if he could get back to the ship.

He had his radio. Bingo, right to the fighter director officer. He asked for vectors to the ship and reported his situation. His compass worked but could he hold a course? The ailerons brought the shredded right wing up. He could hold a course. Thank God, it was now broad daylight.

He tentatively pushed his rudders; they were still jammed. How could the bullets have hit and jammed the rudder without hitting him? He'd skidded left as the bullets came and his hard left rudder had twisted the plane in the air to make it skid, but certainly, the fighter's tail had not been more than 1 foot or so out of the direct line when it was hit. That meant the bullets had passed within 1 foot of his shoulder. Too close! Too close!

Relying on his faithful engine, Gilman neared the fleet in his cocked-up, sliding-sideways airplane, with the shredded right wing, the big flat place where the radome had been, the inoperative rudder and no air speed indicator. Again the question, Could he land aboard? It was his duty to save the plane if possible and, ordinarily, the pilot had a better chance with a deck landing than in a water landing.

As Gilman approached the fleet he tried to put his wheels down. Another blow: his hydraulics had been shot out and the wheels would not extend. Well, he could lower them by hand.

But the flaps? Were they gone too? They were! Now what? Would he dare come aboard without flaps, without rudder, with sloppy ailerons, at a high stalling speed and flying slightly sideways to boot?

Landing aboard was getting to sound hopeless but water landings also had their problems. Well, if the skipper wanted him to try to come aboard, he'd try.

The carriers had been running west while launching the first strike. The farther west they went, the more vulnerable they were to land-based air attack. Now they were heading east at high speed to put more distance between them and the land-based bombers. To take Cobalt 7 aboard, the *Lexington* had to turn around the run west, upwind. The other ships in the fleet had to escort the carrier, so the whole task force—carriers, battleships, cruisers and destroyers—turned around. All turned around together to help John Gilman land. They wanted to make it quick so they could steam east again.

Gilman began his upwind leg of the landing pattern. He came down to 120 feet, slowing his fighter as much as he dared, and began to make his downwind turn. He was flying very carefully, like walking on eggs. He banked cautiously in the turn. At this point, a nervous air control officer let his tension show by telling John to expedite his landing. It was some of the worst advice John had ever received. *Expedite* is a term of urgency. Honest John Gilman, always willing to give his utmost, tried to comply and his whole world blew up.

As he increased his bank and tightened his turn, the poor shattered right wing, with its 2 foot wide flat spot destroying airflow at the end, gave up and stalled. The wing could no longer support the fighter. With a sharp tremor, the plane fell off to the right. It was 120 feet up, about 3 seconds from the water.

Gilman hit full throttle and dropped the nose. He rammed in full aileron to level the plane. The good left wing still had some control; it dropped, leveling the airplane for a split second. Gilman had a burst of elation—they'd make it! Then BAM, the left wing stalled too and the fighter went from a right turn to a violent, near vertical left spin.

Gilman had done everything in the book that he could have. If he still had his rudder, he might have stopped the spin. A good pilot in a trainer can bring his plane through a stall without a spin by quick action with the rudder, moving it first one way then the other, called Walking the Rudder. He would have to be a truly superior pilot to walk a low-wing fighter down without a spin. Here Gilman had no rudder and a damaged aircraft. He spun. Half a second from a horrendous, full-power crash he knew he was a goner.

Falling 120 feet is like bailing out of a twelve-story building and Gilman was at full throttle, fighting for control. There was a violent crash. The plane struck left wing and nose first. The propeller blades flew off the engine in three different directions. A tower of spray hid the airplane. The plane went completely under, took one convulsive bounce backwards so that its tail appeared momentarily, then disappeared and sank.

Grandpa Pettibone, the mythical advice-giving oldest Naval Aviator alive, had much good advice for his pilots. One caution was this: When making a crash-landing on the ocean, don't be too quick to unbuckle your seatbelt and shoulder straps and start to leave. You may have smashed into a wave and skipped right off the wave like a flat stone scaled onto a pond. Because the impact is so hard and because of the spray and the splash immersing you, you may not realize you have bounced, are still in the air and are about to strike the next big wave nose first. Wait for the second hit, laddie, before unbuckling your safety belt, or you may never see home again.

Gilman's rapidly spinning, steeply diving plane never bounced twice. It hit almost straight in and then started down. Gilman had read Grandpa Pettibone and waited for the second bounce. He sat there in his cockpit, hand on the safety belt releases. He was in solid green water, watching the bubbles rise as the plane gathered momentum toward the bottom, thousands of feet below. It dawned on him that there would be no second splash and he should have left some time ago. He released his crash harness, pulled his Mae West inflaters and pushed off for the surface somewhere above him.

Mae Wests were designed in simpler times. They would easily float a fully clothed pilot but as the war progressed the pilots picked up extra baggage. Gilman had strapped to him a .38 revolver with thirty rounds of ammunition, a big knife, a parachute, a jungle survival backpack and a rubber raft. He was wearing heavy, high shoes, originally designed for Marine Infantry, and a long, one-piece flight suit that made swimming extremely difficult.

The old Mae West just wasn't up to keeping him afloat. The life jacket helped, but unless he paddled, he couldn't float high enough to breathe. Not having ditched before, Gilman didn't realize this, and when he released his airplane and pushed off for the surface, he expected to pop right to the top. Instead, he would never reach the surface without strenuous swimming on his own.

Gilman was a good swimmer and he started for the surface. He'd already been underwater for the better part of 1 minute and was becoming conscious of a growing need for air. He swam harder and harder. He needed air more and more. He swam desperately, clawing at the water, trying to get to the surface. Icy cold fear shot through him. He couldn't get air! He needed it now! Desperation swept over him and added its impact to fear. Go, go, go. Panic appeared in the background. He was drowning. Air, how he needed air! He couldn't go on, but he had to. His reflexes kept saying go, go go, but his mind said no, no, no. He struggled further. If panic reached him it would all be over.

Two more hard strokes and he burst through the surface of the ocean and sucked in a glorious breath of air. He paddled for a minute, keeping his head up and breathing in that wonderful, wonderful air. It was difficult to keep his head above water. The waves slapped him and he took in a mouthful of salt water and choked.

He had to get out his raft. It was tough, bouncing around in the waves. He'd pause for a breath, then sink under again and try for it, then come up for another breath and try again. He fumbled with the raft release, and after a few times, released and inflated it. That was a mistake of sorts. With all his gear on, tired from his ordeal and trying to breathe without taking in more salt water, he couldn't climb into the raft. His bulky backpack, his heavy gun, his lead-weight shoes, all conspired against him. Well, he didn't have to climb in. A destroyer was nearby and they'd pick him up. So, physically tired and emotionally spent, he clung to the raft and bobbed up and down in the ocean waiting to be rescued.

He might have discarded some of his gear to get into the raft. He considered releasing the survival backpack but it didn't seem worth the effort. Besides, he wasn't rescued yet and he might need it if the ship missed him.

He could have thrown his gun away but he was nervous about sharks. They were in this area. As each wave approached, he studied it carefully, half expecting to see the big, sinister shape of a man-eating shark staring at him from within. He'd keep his gun. He'd heard that when a shark came near you, sometimes it would turn away if you fired your gun underwater.

Within ½ hour, a destroyer eased up to him, lowered a cargo net to climb out on, sent two swimmers to help him and pulled him aboard. Gilman was aboard the destroyer about 24 hours, and from all the adrenaline he'd pumped into his system, he shook the whole time.

Destroyer life was not carrier life. It was a normal day at sea. The carrier cruised along with no perceptible pitch or roll but the destroyer rolled from side to side, so that Gilman had to hang on all the time. On every wave, the whole bow of the ship would lift out of the water as it steamed along. The pitching was even harder to get used to than the rolling. The bow would go up, and then when it started down, there would be that sinking, fluttering feeling in your stomach. Gilman came down for breakfast the next day, ordered two fried eggs, took one look at them and ran for the head to throw up.

That afternoon, the destroyer pulled up to the portside near the stern of the carrier, rigged a breaches buoy and sent Gilman back to his ship. The canvas chair was returned to the destroyer with Gilman's ransom: 8 gallons of ice cream for the sailors who rescued him.

A few weeks later, John Gilman was ordered detached from the *Lexington* to return to the States. He was flown to Manus Island, an assembly point for crews awaiting transportation to the States. He and a friend were standing in a chow line at lunchtime when the friend said, "John would you like to meet the pilot who shot you down? I know him. He's standing right over there."

They did go over. The meeting was brief and cool. The pilot was chagrined.

No phrases were uttered that would live in history or that could adequately express the feelings of the participants.

Chapter 19

The final act

Late October 1944 saw the start of the Japanese suicide attacks. The Kamikaze Corps, the Divine Wind, was created to stop the US fleet with the concept of one man's life for one ship. The attacks started slowly then rolled like a wave. Eventually, thousands of Japanese pilots were training to sacrifice themselves.

We shot them down by the hundreds but still they came. It wasn't like any battle anyone could relate to. They didn't break and run, no matter that their attack was shattered and decimated. To stop them, you had to kill them. You had to kill them all, and when one was blasted from the sky, another was right behind him.

The Divine Wind first blew on the *Intrepid* on October 29, 1944, near midday.

The bullhorn thundered, "General quarters! General quarters! All Hands to battle stations!" The Klaxon added anxiety and speeded running footsteps with its insistent *"BRACK! BRACK! BRACK!"*

I raced to the ready room, and as I reached it, I heard the squawker calling the approach of a bogey. I heard the destroyers of the screen start firing, then, closer to us, the big ships opened up and then our own ship's guns began firing.

Every size gun is distinctive. The 20 millimeter automatic cannons rattle and bang like bigger-than-life machine guns. The 40 millimeters are in quads, four guns to a mount, synchronized. The two inside fire, then the two outside fire. They have a rhythm that talks to you like red-hot jazz. The 5 inchers go *BLAM! BLAM!* The ship shakes and if you're on deck the concussion seems to lift you up with each explosion. With each shot, a yellow ball of flame bursts from the gun barrel and you feel the flash of radiated heat on your face.

The 20 millimeters line each side of the catwalks along the edge of the flight deck. In 1944, segregation was still a part of life. Our food servers were black men. When the ship was in combat, they were assigned to safety and obscurity in the galley below decks. This was galling to them, and they made a special request to the captain that they be allowed to fight, as well as serve in the wardroom. The messmen were given a gun tub of six 20 millimeter cannons, to man and fight.

As I sat in the ready room that day listening to the guns, there came a larger sound, like that of a muffled thunderclap. It lasted only 1 second but it shuddered the ship. We'd been hit!

Sirens rolled and the bullhorn blatted. "Fire! Fire! Fire in the port gun tubs! Damage control! Damage control! CORPSMEN! CORPSMEN!"

137

A kamikaze plane had hit the messmen's gun tub. The firing ceased; the bogey had been alone. I ducked out of the ready room and onto the catwalk. There was the gun tub, full of dead men. No bomb had gone off. The fire had been from the plane's fuel and was being brought under control. The corpsmen were taking two burned, dead men from the tub. As I stuck my head up a corpsman was pulling on the arm of a dead messman and the skin of his burned arm just slid off in the corpsman's hands.

The smell of death and burned flesh was searing. I started to leave, just get away, but as I did I saw the guns in the tub. One gun had been hit by the plane and lay at a crazy angle. Every other gun in the tub was pointing in the exact same direction, almost straight up, right at where the incoming plane had been. The gunners were still strapped in their guns, all dead. Every single one had died at his gun firing at the kamikaze. The next day ten messmen were buried at sea. The whole ship took pride in their steadfast last stand.

Kamikazes became a way of life. It was eerie to fight a foe where every attacker, down to the last man, had to be killed before he reached you or *he* got *you.*

We'd fought up and down the far Pacific from Davao, on Mindanao, in the south, to Formosa and to Okinawa, near Japan, in the north. The pilots knew the big one—the attack on Japan itself—would come soon. Japan's best men and planes were waiting there. Could our ships survive fanatical attacks of the kamikaze all the way to Japan, right into the home islands, and then meet the first team? It gave me a scary feeling to think about it.

November 25, 1944, redoubled our concern. In that one day, the kamikazes crashed on three of our big carriers and the bombs and fires put all three out of action. The ships survived but were lost to the fleet for crucial months.

This was the worst day ever for the *Intrepid.* The ship was hit by kamikazes and was gutted by fire and bombs, and sixty-two men died on her decks and another forty died of wounds thereafter.

At that time, the *Intrepid* was a part of Task Force 38.2, steaming side by side with her sister ship the *Hancock.* The medium carriers *Cabot* and *Independence* were also part of the task force. The carriers were escorted by the new superbattleship *New Jersey*, with Adm. William "Bull" Halsey aboard, plus the battleship *Iowa*, and by cruisers and destroyers galore.

The carriers were preparing to launch strikes against shipping in the seas of southern Luzon. The two big carriers were maneuvering like twins. On signal, they turned into the wind together and started launching their first strikes. As I sat in my dive-bomber on the *Intrepid*'s deck, waiting to move forward, I looked across at the *Hancock* and could see her dive-bombers turning up their engines and waiting to move forward on her deck. As my skipper took off, so did theirs.

I jockeyed slowly forward and so did my counterpart in the dive-bomber on the *Hancock.* I arrived at the takeoff spot on deck and so did my counterpart on the *Hancock.*

At that moment, all hell broke loose. "General quarters! General quarters! Man your battle stations!" The Klaxon blared, sirens yipped, men ran and guns started firing everywhere. We were under a surprise attack, and I was sitting in the center of the deck in the middle of the action, completely exposed, immobile, helpless and the aiming point of the kamikaze.

Overhead, the kamikaze pilot could look down on a sea full of our ships. He could pick any one of them for his target, but his final instructions, for his final flight, for his suicide plunge for his emperor, had been "Get the carriers!"

He now had two of the big ones below him. He could strike for Japan at either one. He'd put his bomb, his plane and himself right into the center of a carrier. Which one? He chose the ship on the right. He made his attack. I could see him coming. He was hit, flames poured from his wings, but he kept coming. The flames spread outward. He looked like a comet, but he came on straight as a die. He hit the center of the deck at the takeoff spot but on the *Hancock* not the *Intrepid.* He crashed directly into my counterpart on the ship on the right and both planes and both crews disintegrated on that deck in a tremendous explosion of flame and fire.

I lived only because, by chance, he dove on the ship to his right instead of the one to his left.

On the *Intrepid,* when the kamikaze had been spotted overhead, the bullhorn bellowed "Commence firing! Commence firing!" and then "Cease launching aircraft." The ship lay over to starboard as it began a high-speed emergency turn to port.

On the *Hancock* the fires raged. Thick black smoke poured from every opening. Orange tongues of flame flashed and flickered in the rolling smoke. The *Intrepid* would be next.

A kamikaze diving on Essex. National Archives

The kamikaze hits Hancock. Hancock, *sister of and steaming beside* Intrepid, *is hit while launching planes. The dive-bomber in the launch spot is blown to bits. The author, in the launch spot on the* Intrepid, *watched this and then made the unauthorized takeoff to get off that deck and airborne.* National Archives

I had to get off that deck or be killed on it. My place was in the air, not here. The order to cease launching planes be damned! I revved up the engine to full power and let her go. I thundered down the deck as the ship turned and then up and away into the relative safety of the air.

We now had only four bombers airborne and could expect none from the *Hancock*. However, the ships' radarscopes were again clear of bogeys, so the *Intrepid* came back into the wind and continued launching. Before long, we had our strike of twelve bombers and the fighter escorts, joined up and ready to depart for the shores of Luzon.

We were shaken by having seen our sister ship hit with that tremendous explosion, and our fellow dive-bombers savaged on her decks. At a time like that, what you have seen tests your power to comprehend. You don't usually see planes shot down in flames, crashing around you or a gigantic ship with thousands of men aboard burning and exploding.

In the past you may have struggled and fought for victory. For example, in football you've given your best and greatest effort to win. But this is different. This game is for keeps! The stakes and losses are infinitely greater; simply, they are life or death. It's not the movies. That billion dollar ship is really going down. It's our ship and our men and they are not coming back!

You look again, grit your teeth and fly toward the enemy, grimly determined to wipe him from the face of the earth.

We didn't know it then but we were never to fly again from the decks of the *Intrepid*.

We set our course for the Philippines.

A scout had reported four Jap ships in a protected bay off the island of Marinduque, in the North Sibuyan Sea, south of Manila. They were warships, long and sleek, destroyers of some type. The mission of such ships was to transport men and ammunition from Luzon to the Japanese forces fighting our men on Leyte. Their tactics were to wait for dark, then run down the island chain to reinforce and supply their troops. They chose not to move in daylight, when we were in the area.

Often, the destroyers used for these missions were old or obsolete, but they were still fast warships; they had to be to make the run to Leyte, unload and be safely away from the battle zone by dawn. During the day, they'd seek a sheltered cove or even tie up to an island and cover themselves with camouflage and nets if possible. According to Japanese records, these four ships had left Ormoc Bay near manila on November 24, 1944. The first night they reached Marinduque Island and hid in a bay. The record shows that there were 3,470 soldiers and sailors aboard. The record further states that, of all those men, only ten survived.

Two of the four ships had been attacked and sunk by VB-18's first strike of the day. Now, an hour later, we were after the remaining two. We had six 1,000 pound packages to deliver to each ship. There were 1,670 men on those two ships—not one survived.

Our scout plane had reported the correct position and we navigated right to the island. The day was clear and the sun was high in the sky. We came over the island at 14,000 feet and flew slightly past the ships to be directly up-sun from them. The ships were slender, not easy to hit, but they were at anchor.

Six bombers attacked each ship. At the chosen point, the first bomber pulled up in a smooth, soaring, graceful wingover; rolled inverted; and started down. Each following bomber pulled up, over and down, almost in cadence. We came directly out of the sun. The AA fire was minimal. After the first thousand-pounder went off, either on or right beside the ship, the AA fire, if anymore came, was ineffectual. A 1,000 pound bomb exploding on a light ship destroys the ship and disables its crew.

This day each ship took six 1,000 pound bomb hits or near misses. The ships disappeared in the smoke and fire of the bomb blasts and the 100 foot tall geysers of water from the near misses. When the smoke and spume cleared away, the ships were gone. They had been blown to pieces and sunk in about one minute! There was no trace of the crews. They died, all of them. 1,670 men died without even a chance to radio they were under attack. As far as the Japanese knew, they just disappeared.

Once more I was appalled at the devastation of the ships and the complete annihilation of so many men. Yet, I felt like cheering each time a bomb hit home. But then I shuddered as bomb after bomb exploded with fearful intensity, sending forth shattering shock waves and flying shrapnel that churned the water. In a sense it was unreal and impersonal. I saw the ships being blown apart but I couldn't picture the violent deaths of the men aboard them.

I thought how close it had been today. Had the kamikaze pilot who'd crashed on the *Hancock* an hour before started his dive 100 yards to his left, he might have struck the *Intrepid* instead, and then I would have been dead, this strike would not have taken off, and these Japanese would have been alive and free to continue fighting our men on Leyte. How close they had come to success. How close I had come to death—again.

Japanese destroyers at anchor in protected cove, just after first bombs have fallen. The first ship is already burning and listing. USN/W. A. Brown via Ben Emge

A few seconds later the ships are smothered in the blasts. Ben Emge (plane in lower right corner) pulls out after a direct hit. Only the tips of bows of the ships are still showing. USN/W. A. Brown via Ben Emge

As the bombers completed their dives, they met to the north to leave for home together, but I had a job to do. My rear gunner carried a camera to record the results of our attacks. So when I pulled out of the bomb run, I circled the targets while he took pictures. It was the only way the Air Combat Intelligence officers could be sure that we had done what we said. We took four pictures. They were graphic and are now part of Navy archives.

After the photo passes, I caught up to the group as it started back for the *Intrepid.*

Twenty minutes later, the radio squawked, we were ordered to change course and proceed to Leyte Island and land at Tacloban airstrip there. No reason was given, but we knew. Our ship had been hit or sunk, and we were on our own.

Leyte was the only Allied airfield within range. We were off on a new adventure. We turned south, flying down toward the southern tip of Luzon. The countryside, when we could see it, was table flat. There were clouds now, dark, gray, higher layers and sort of raggedy, rolling, gray, lower layers with the tops at 8,000 or 9,000 feet. We flew among and occasionally through them. The gray misty clouds were depressing and sinister. The lower levels were almost black.

I was looking uneasily off to the right and ahead and became more and more aware that the thicket of clouds we were about to pass had strange characteristics. Its lower part, which I could only glimpse occasionally through the other clouds, was very dark, eerie and threatening. Its middle

The remains of the first ship blow up while 1,000 pounders disintegrate the second ship. Fantastic dive-bombing. USN/W. A. Brown via Ben Emge

All that marks the ships are the widening ripples on the water and puffs of smoke and steam in the air. The ships are gone and all the crews and troops are dead. Hundreds of men died in about 90 seconds. USN/W. A. Brown via Ben Emge

part rose smoothly at the start but changed to a curling roll, much like a wave at the beginning of rapids in a deep river, where the current passes over a huge rock and breaks behind it.

Rock! My God, that was it! That cloud was wrapped around a mountain! A lone mountain peak rising out of table-flat land, a mountain peak 8,000 feet high where we expected nothing. The clouds were forming on its upwind side, rising to its peak and streaming off downwind like a deep current of water rolling over rocks in a rapid. It was right off our wing tips. Was it the only mountain around? Were cones of rock hidden in these other clouds? Had the flight leader seen this? Let's go for more altitude!

I looked back at the mountain. I saw a symmetrical cone—no jagged peaks or rocky spurs, just smooth even sides: a perfect cone. It was Mount Mayon, a single volcanic cone springing alone from the flatland of southern Luzon. Breathtaking!

On we flew toward Leyte, the only base we could reach. Without it we would lose all our planes by water landings at sea. How close we had come.

Tacloban airstrip at Leyte was on the fringe of the ground war and a focal point of the air war. A thousand ships and landing craft lay off or steamed beyond Leyte's beaches. Japanese air attacks were almost constant day and night, usually concentrating on the ships and beaches rather than on the perimeter of the airstrip where we camped with the Army.

On Nov. 25, 1944, at about 1130 hours a kamikaze evades a Hellcat and dives on the ship. USN via A. V. Daschke

The kamikaze is hit and burning but comes on.

The airstrip was made of flat, perforated steel sections that locked together. As we arrived over the base, the air control officer warned us to use extreme caution on landing; the steel paving was narrow and gave braking action different from that of any surface we knew. He suggested that any plane that came off the steel mat at any speed but idle would probably ground loop and damage itself and others.

I came around for a landing in my turn. I was flying heads-up, cautiously and with plenty of adrenaline flowing. The runway wasn't as wide as the ship, and planes were parked along its entire length, many only feet back from the mat. The mat looked wavy and slippery—no place for a hard landing.

With great care and deep respect for my surroundings I greased the bomber in and gingerly braked as I rolled down the mat. I cleared the runway and looked around.

Army P-38 fighters and an assortment of reconnaissance planes were all over, but almost everywhere I looked was a Navy carrier type—fighter or bomber—junked! The planes were obviously roughly bulldozed back out of the way. They were bent, twisted, resting at odd angles and pushed into piles against each other in a sobering scene. What could have caused this mayhem? What disaster had befallen our forces that twenty aircraft were lost in one calamity?

We were greeted by an Army officer who would find space for us and who was a fountain of information. A few weeks back a carrier had been hit. As we were, the airborne strike was ordered to Tacloban, but it was before

The kamikaze strikes the Intrepid. *USN via Intrepid Museum*

Another view of the kamikaze strike on the Intrepid. National Archives

Sailors on New Jersey *watch* Intrepid *burn and explode.* National Archives

the steel landing mats were in place. The planes had landed on graded sand. They had been unable to brake and when their wheels caught in the sand they became uncontrollable. Only three survived in flyable condition. The rest of the planes were bulldozed to the side lines so that the mat could be laid and the Army could operate its planes. How close we had come.

As for the *Intrepid*, it had been hit by kamikazes. It was still underway but burning fiercely and was reported to be at the base of a black column of smoke 1 mile high. The outcome was still in doubt.

We'd seen the *Hancock* hit, the *Intrepid* was now burning, and on the same day, the *Essex* was heavily damaged and knocked out of the war until repaired.

In one day, the Japanese kamikazes had crippled three of our big, first-line, fast carriers. The ships could be months in repairs. Could the kamikazes stop our drive to Japan? Could they drive us from the Philippines? Without carriers, we couldn't advance—Hell, we couldn't even support the advances already made. Our group looked grimly at each other.

We stayed two days in Leyte, long enough to get dysentery and to thank our lucky stars for our shipboard accommodations. The Army people were great. They made us feel like honored guests. They shared their warm Australian beer, their mosquito repellants and their mess kits with us.

The fires start and the crew fights the flames for their lives. USN via Intrepid Museum

The Intrepid *burning fiercely.* National Archives

I commented to an officer on their fortitude in living under such rigorous conditions. The officer laughed and said, "This is a headquarters company, it is luxury. You should see how the troops at the front live."

The front was "just over the hill." The P–38s flew close air support for the ground troops all day. Frequently, their missions were only 10 minutes long: load up, fly over the ridge, dump the bombs and rockets, dodge antiaircraft and fly back for more. A hazardous way to earn a living.

We received our orders to move the second day. We were to fuel up and fly to Babelthuap in the Palaus, fuel again and fly to Ulithi Atoll, the gathering place of the fleet.

Our first leg was 600 miles over open ocean. All our planes were single-engine and there wasn't a pontoon in the group.

The airstrip at Babelthuap was uncrowded and primitive. As I jockeyed my plane toward the takeoff spot there, I looked at stumps of coconut trees and rocks, bulldozed to the side of the runway during construction.

The fighters took off first. It was going well. This was the last leg of the trip, and with the ship damaged, this might be the last flight for all of us before going home. I thought, *Just be careful now! Don't let anything happen now!*

A fighter revved up and started down the runway. He was rolling, about to take off, when for no apparent reason his left tire blew out. The Hellcat swerved to the left. "Keep it on the runway!" I implored. "For God sake, keep it on the runway!"

The Intrepid *is hit a second time on Nov. 25, 1944. The fires rage and tremendous explosions shake the ship, only her bow is visible as the* New Jersey, *with Admiral Halsey aboard, looks on helplessly.* USN

Four of the Intrepid's *crew are buried at sea.* USN via Intrepid Museum

The pilot tried, but the plane skidded off the runway at 60 miles per hour and into the area of stumps and rocks. The fighter had a big stream-lined auxiliary gas tank hung below the fuselage, full of gasoline. The stumps seemed to reach out, to tear at the tank and try to explode the plane. Miraculously, none hit the tank—when *Whamo!* The tank hit a rock and was torn asunder. The plane, still rolling, was engulfed in flame and a towering blast of black smoke.

I sat stunned. This was the last hop before home. It wasn't even combat. Just a short ferry hop and we'd be there. What an awful way to go. I felt sick, heartsick, drained. Who was it? Which pilot? Which friend?

The flight continued taking off. Plane after plane rolled down the runway past the burning fighter and on its way, each pilot depressed or angry, depending on his personality. I flew toward Ulithi, depressed and upset with the unfairness of such a bad break.

We approached Ulithi, a huge harbor, ringed by miles of long reef and a few tiny islands. Ships stretched to the horizon and there, on the rear edge, was the *Intrepid*. The skipper saw her too and led the formation, thirty-six planes, toward the ship. We'd fly over it, our last salute to our ship.

An OS2U, a float plane from a cruiser, was heading for the *Intrepid* from our right. The plane was in a right turn, the pilot looking away from us, rubbernecking the ship. That plane was on a collision course, with a thirty-six-plane formation!

We couldn't turn sharply enough to avoid him. Our leader put the formation into a shallow, but then increasingly steep, dive. All thirty-six planes followed but the float plane wanted a closer look so he started down. The more we went down the more he did. Would he look around? I was

Intrepid under attack again on Apr. 16, 1945. Note two kamikazes diving on the ship from the right. USN via Intrepid Museum

The Intrepid *has been hit.* USN via Intrepid Museum

A near miss by a kamikaze. USN via Intrepid Museum

152

A kamikaze crashes close aboard. USN via Intrepid Museum

The Intrepid *burning on Apr. 16, 1945, but underway at full speed. Note waterfalls from firefighting pouring off the hangar deck as ship lists from the turn.* USN via Intrepid Museum

angry and scared at the looming tragedy. "Look around, damn it, look around!"

It was our last hop. He'd take out four or five planes if he didn't look around! He never did. He came right into the formation from the right side. The key section leaders had seen him coming, and in the last few seconds, the top sections of our formation pulled up and scattered and the lower sections dove steeply and scattered and he missed us all!

I was shaking from anger at the near miss, and on our last hop! But, we'd had a reprieve; we were lucky. If only we hadn't lost the fighter on takeoff.

We came around and landed on the little coral island and climbed out of the planes. I stood with a small group of pilots and watched the torpedo bombers roll up, swing around and stop. Our skipper walked over to their leader for a moment and then came back with great news. The pilot of the plane that had gone off the runway and burned on takeoff was able to get out. He was unhurt, he was picked up by one of the torpedo bombers, they brought him along and he rejoined our ranks. Another wonderful break. I was flooded with feelings of thankfulness and relief, the feelings one has when a man you saw die returns to his brothers.

Another kamikaze is shot down. USN via Intrepid Museum

The USS Bunker Hill *was struck by two kamikaze planes within 30 minutes on May 11, 1945.* USN via R. F. Dorr

Chapter 20

Homeward bound

A boat from the *Intrepid* met us at the coral runway at Ulithi and ferried us back to the ship. The ship was riding level in the water but we could see her injuries as we approached. The areas above the hangar deck were blackened from fire and smoke. She had a gaping hole in her flight deck, which sagged on twisted and blackened steel beams. She smelled of fire and death, a sickening smell.

The ship had been attacked by kamikaze planes. The ship and the screen had shot them down, one after another as they had come on. Finally, one penetrated the wall of antiaircraft fire and crashed through the flight

VB–18 Helldivers at Ulithi after kamikaze attack set the Intrepid *on fire. VB–18 bid goodbye to its planes on Ulithi—a boat carried them to the* Intrepid. *USN via Intrepid Museum*

deck and into a ready room just under it. The ready room was the battle station of a dozen of the ship's men and all were killed.

The firefighters and damage control people had been safe within the armored superstructure of the island of the ship. After the bomb hit, they had poured forth fighting the flames and smoke, then almost without warning, a second plane had smashed into the *Intrepid*. The crews were wiped out. Fifty men had died in the blast and forty more died later from injuries.

Among the dead was our flight surgeon, Dr. John Fish, our chief parachute rigger, Tom Hanley, and our leading chief petty officer, Lumpkin Wood. Their battle station was the parachute loft, a compartment near the flight deck. They had suffocated from the smoke and fumes of the fires.

The fires had been fed by gasoline from the ship's own planes, caught on deck in the spreading flames.

The crew had reorganized itself and had fought the fires heroically, for hours, finally saving the ship.

After the fires were out, orders came to send the *Intrepid* back to Hawaii and then to San Francisco for repairs. The dive-bomber and torpedo squadrons were to go back with her. Tremendously exciting! I was being sent home, I had survived! I'd see my family again! I had a life ahead of me again! The excitement and anticipation were like those of a small boy the week before Christmas.

We were going home but our fighter squadron wasn't. In response to the kamikaze attacks and to prepare for the invasion of Japan, the Navy was increasing the number of fighters each ship would carry. The fighters were to leave us, go to another ship and continue the war. We'd worked

At Ulithi pilots have a beer. They're hoping they're starting for home. Front row: Duckett, Chauvel, Ehrke; second row: Emge, Keane, Chaney, Anderson; third row: McIntosh, Serrell. USN via A. V. Daschke

hand-in-glove with them for months. They'd protected us and risked their lives for us. We hated to see them go.

The least we could do was give them one hell of a sendoff. We had a liquor mess; before leaving Pearl Harbor we'd pooled our funds and laid in a year's supply of alcoholic substances. We weren't allowed to drink on the ship (but we did some anyway) and now we were going home early with our supply hardly dented. The fighters, the bombers and the torpedos determined to dent the supply on this occasion.

The action lasted only a couple hours. In the annals of the Navy, this party's intensity may have been equaled but was never surpassed.

Fighting 18 went over the side and down the gangplank in the most inebriated whiskey haze in which any squadron had ever left a ship. My hangover lasted two days—but it was the least I could do to show my appreciation for our fighter squadron.

The following morning, we all watched as the winches hauled in the ship's immense chain and mammoth anchor. We were on our way to Hawaii and then to San Francisco, and then for me, to Rochester, New York.

The Pacific is so vast. Hawaii is actually closer to New York City than it is to the Philippines.

For days, we steamed east at high speed. We airmen stood no watches, flew no planes, had no briefings. We played a little cards and we walked around and thought a lot. The war sunk in as it never had while we were doing it. In the war zone, if you lost a wingman, the loss didn't hit you; you

Gunner Daschke practicing "survival." USN via A. V. Daschke

Gunner Dick Shipman without his plane. USN via R. Shipman

protected yourself from it. I thought it was like an introduction in reverse: you knew him, then he was gone and then you didn't know him.

As the ship sped eastward day after day the war regurgitated into my mind. I was "reintroduced" to my dead friends. I remembered them. I remembered that I knew and liked them and that it was a tragedy when they died. The thoughts were haunting and I had to keep my thinking and especially my emotions under tight rein. It was a disturbing passage.

Finally, two glorious days in Hawaii and then on to the Golden Gate. Two wild and wonderful days in San Francisco, then on to Rochester by air.

I'd traveled 8,000 miles from Ulithi, then 60 miles west of Rochester, at Buffalo, New York, the plane would go no farther. Rochester was snowed in. I had to get home that day, I had to! The Greyhound buses still ran. I grabbed my duffle bag, ran to the bus stop and made the last 60 miles on the bus. I walked through the door of our house at 9:00 p.m. on Christmas Eve. I'd made it!

The joy of my father and brothers was unbounded. The joy of my mother, transcendent.

John F. Forsyth in 1945. USN

Epilogue

There can be nothing worse than war. The phrase sounds trite. We've heard it before. Do we pass it by with a furtive, sidelong glance, reluctant to dig out our deeply suppressed experiences? War is bitterness. Four hundred thousand men, the best in America, killed. Wasted. Slaughtered. Cut down, blasted, burned, torn and disfigured. Left to rot in jungles and European dung holes; washed onto hard coral atolls, bloated and gone, with the waves pushing up a little sand drift on their sea side. No more sunshine, love or family for them.

The waste is incomprehensible.

Five million dollars worth of overage ammunition dumped into the Pacific from one ship on one day to make room for new, which may shoot a few yards closer to the target. A $500 million ship sunk to the bottom in minutes. The infantryman who steps on a mine. The flash of flame, the puff of smoke and the smear of blood on the leaves nearby. The pilot—"They shot down Andy!—God, damn them!—God, bless him!—God, pity his mother!"

The Marine ahead, your buddy in school. You knew him laughing in the classrooms, and in football charging shoulder to shoulder with you, full and hard, together, smashing and driving as a team into the brawny tackle opposite. You didn't dare think that when the 20 millimeters shot his middle out, sprayed you with his blood, and he gurgled and died as you ran past.

Can we who call ourselves veterans, and we who know all this, still steel ourselves against it? We can't bury all this only to let another generation steel themselves to forget a similar chapter in their lives. Take out that picture of your brother in arms and look at it. Recall who he was before, and what a person he was. He's dead now, stopped in his tracks. We've worked at forgetting but we should remember. Remember the terrible wastefulness of war. We should bring to our minds the cost in numbers, figure it in personalities, that of the friendly lad or the rough buddy we knew and lost.

The cost is unbearable.

We've done a lot, but we can do more. We can still help to prevent another war. Look at your pictures and think on it. Make your views known. Support a strong defense, make it clear that the price of aggression will be too high to pay.

Make the United Nations work! As Sir Brian Urqhart of the UN has said, "We have developed the art of war to the point we really can't use it. We must use the United Nations. The UN alternative makes nonviolent use of an international force of soldiers, a catalyst for peace rather than an instrument of war. It is a powerful idea, an evolutionary step toward an alternative system to war."

Support this or a program of your own, but act! There's a fight to be won! Move out! Man your planes!